# STREET CORNER TALKING

## THE AUTOBIOGRAPHY OF KIM SIMMONDS

# STREET CORNER TALKING
## THE AUTOBIOGRAPHY OF KIM SIMMONDS

### THE LIFE AND MUSIC OF THE FOUNDER AND GUITARIST OF SAVOY BROWN

WITH DEBBIE LYONS SIMMONDS
FOREWORD BY MIKE VERNON, MBE

4880 Lower Valley Road • Atglen, PA 19310

**Other Schiffer books**

*Fleetwood Mac in Chicago: The Legendary Chess Blues Session, January 4, 1969*, Jeff Lowenthal and Robert Schaffner, 978-0-7643-6495-2

*Cream: Clapton, Bruce & Baker Sitting on Top of the World, San Francisco, February–March 1968*, Edoardo Genzolini, 978-0-7643-6592-8

*Richard Manuel: His Life and Music, from the Hawks and Bob Dylan to The Band*, Stephen T. Lewis, 978-0-7643-6924-7



Library of Congress Control Number: 2025939853



Designed by Jack Chappell
Cover design by Molly Shields
Type set in Cheddar Gothic / Pill Gothic / Times
Front cover photo courtesy of Jim Summaria

ISBN: 978-0-7643-7101-1
ePub: 978-1-5073-0646-8
Printed in China
10 9 8 7 6 5 4 3 2 1

Published by Schiffer Publishing, Ltd.
4880 Lower Valley Road
Atglen, PA 19310
Phone: (610) 593-1777; Fax: (610) 593-2002
Email: Info@schifferbooks.com
Web: www.schifferbooks.com

# CONTENTS

# FOREWORD

## by Mike Vernon, MBE

Formed in the autumn months of 1965 by guitarist and founder Kim Simmonds, the Savoy Brown Blues Band was fast becoming a firm favorite in and around the burgeoning Blues Club scene in central and suburban London. They had a residency at "Kilroy's" in Battersea, South London, and that's where I was to finally meet the band in the early part of 1966. In those early days the band was composed of Brice Portius (vocals), Kim Simmonds (guitar), Martin Stone (guitar), John O'Leary (harp), Bob Hall (piano), Ray Chappell (bass), and Leo Mannings (drums). "Kilroy's" was upstairs above the Nag's Head (long since demolished) and was very well attended.

My recall is that, following the show, I talked briefly with both Kim and his brother Harry and made plans to meet as soon as possible. Harry was acting as a booking agent and had an office up the hill from "Kilroy's" near to Queenstown Road Railway Station. He was not only booking bands but was also managing Kim's outfit. We met at his office and talked—a lot! I explained to the two of them that I was working as an assistant to the head of A&R department at the Decca Record Company Ltd., only 2 miles away in Lambeth.

For two years or so, my brother Richard and I, along with Neil Slaven, had been publishing a fanzine known as *R&B Monthly*. I think both Kim and Harry were aware of that fact and that we were also operating a fledgling Blues Record label, Blue Horizon. They were soon to be told that that label was really interested in recording and releasing a single of Savoy Brown's Blues Band—note the band name change. I explained that releases on Purdah—part of Blue Horizon—would be limited but pressings would be increased if there was sufficient interest from blues fans. At that moment in time, I believe that the first release featuring T. S. McPhee (of John Lee's Groundhogs fame) was already on sale; the second release was to feature John Mayall and Eric Clapton. We agreed to go ahead with making the record and releasing it during the autumn of 1966. Indeed, Purdah 45-3503, "I Tried" b/w "Can't Quit You Baby," was recorded during August 1966 and released on October 11 of that same year; so it says in the *Blue Horizon Records Newsletter*, edition 2, dated September 24. It proved to be an excellent seller.

There can be no doubt that the two Simmonds were the driving force behind this band. Savoy Brown's Blues Band's fame was growing day by day, and I was becoming ever more aware that perhaps I should be looking to record them again, but not for a small and fledgling label. Why not offer the band to my full-time employer—Decca. I suggested to my fellow producer, Neil Slaven, that he visit "Kilroy's" to catch the band's show and then report back to me; a second opinion in favor would be a sensible way to determine which road to follow. Neil returned and the die was cast, although getting the contract signed was not to be a smooth-running event, so said Kim, on Harry's behalf!

The actual recording process of the band's first album, *Shake Down*, was marginally easier. I had already worked on two John Mayall albums for Decca—among many others—and had, once again, asked for Gus Dudgeon to be made available to handle the engineering chores. The band members were really keen to record as one unit, and it may well be that that was how it went. But I do have to say that my "little gray cells" fail me on this one.

On the album sleeve notes, Neil Slaven states that "Savoy Brown are a damn fine band." He also notes that when he first visited the Nags Head to check out the band, it was like "walking into a wall of sound. They had a meaty, full-blooded sound and a "Banzai" attack (approach). They simply reached out and wrung the approval out of you." The album finally saw the light of day in September 1967.

Perhaps now is the time to talk about producer/musician relationships—a touchy subject for some! The end of 1967 and the whole of 1968 was an unbelievably busy period in my life. I was in the throes of launching the Blue Horizon label with the help of distribution via CBS London. We were to sign three new acts—Fleetwood Mac, the Chicken Shack, and Aynsley Dunbar's Retaliation. Understandably, I did not want to lose my highly valued position at Decca, so I decided to approach my then head of department to find a way out to this conundrum. The ultimatum was to be a dismissal or a resignation—I chose the latter on the understanding that I would sign an independent production deal with Decca for five years where I would offer artists to the company before recording them for Blue Horizon. Done and dusted. However, I don't think that I had given sufficient thought as to how I was going to arrange my diary! Social events for me became nothing short of disasters—like a true professional, I put my workload ahead of all else. Whenever I met with John Mayall or Peter Green, it was to discuss the next album or single project. It was to be the same with Kim.

"Out with the old and in with the new" as four members of the original Savoy Brown Band were replaced by vocalist Chris Youlden, guitarist Dave Peverett, a.k.a. "Lonesome Dave," bassist Rivers Jobe, and drummer Roger Earl. I never asked Kim where he found these new and talented musicians, but the oral difference was immediately obvious; in particular, Youlden's husky and very soulful vocals helped create a far more commercial unit.

Spring 1968 and I was back into the Decca No. 2 Studio in London's West Hampstead to record a new album with the now-named Savoy Brown. *Getting to the Point* proved to be an enormous step forward in terms of credibility and, accordingly, received good reviews in the press. By now I was working for both Decca and Blue Horizon—crazy times indeed, but both wearing and rewarding too. I guess you could say that this was to be my vocational lifestyle for the foreseeable future—little or no socializing and lots of work!

October 1968 soon came around, and I was busy booking more studio time for the band to record enough material for singles and a third album. I also recall having a few "acoustic" rehearsals with both Kim and Chris; we also spent time discussing potential arrangements for a small horn session to "dress up" one or two of the new songs. Enter Terry Noonan—trumpeter and musical director. For the life of me, I cannot recall who introduced me to this charming man and accomplished musician—maybe someone reading this will stand up? He proved time and time again to be invaluable on projects where his talents as an arranger can still be heard to this day. He worked with me for a couple of years—Fleetwood Mac, the Web, Chicken Shack, Champion Jack Dupree, Martha Velez, Top Topham, Dana Gillespie, and Christine McVie (née Perfect). And of course, Savoy Brown on three of their albums.

If we backtrack slightly to those "acoustic rehearsals," we can discuss (not in detail, though) the thoughts and ideas we had regarding a horn arrangement for "Train to Nowhere." Again, my memory fails me as to who was the person to come up with this potential idea. If I put money on the table, then I have to say the most likely culprit would have been "yours truly"! It almost always worked out like that. I am also certain that I met up with Terry at his home in South London to run over the projected ideas, every possibility being that either Chris or Kim also attended that day. The haunting and insisting melody is very basic, but it fits like a glove and helped make that song a favorite on radio in the States. The album *Blue Matter* was released during May 1969 in the UK. The US release was made available several months before; in fact, probably at the time we began production on the follow-up, *A Step Further*.

Once again, we collectively made the decision to make use of Terry Noonan's arranging talents—especially notable on "Life's One Act Play" and "Bamboo Grove." I say "collectively" since I have no recall of being involved in any discussions or meetings with band members and Terry regarding this process. Perhaps Terry was given a "free hand" to do as he saw fit? I don't recall . . . once again, "gray-cell failure"! This album was to be my last production with Savoy Brown (sigh) and, I have to say, the most enjoyable. It was also to be the band's first US chart success, reaching #71 on the album charts. A cool way to go out, one could say.

I made friends with both Tone Stevens and Roger Earl—often seen together (with me and Joe Jammer) at the Speakeasy on Margaret Street—near to the BBC headquarters. Great place to relax and listen to good "live" music after a long day in the studio. Sadly, we lost contact in 1970 (or thereabouts). Tone, Roger, and Dave formed Foghat in 1971 and were to become enormously successful in the USA and Canada. I have very fond memories of partying with Tone and Roger—fun days. Chris Youlden and

I got together to make music with engineer Bob Ross down in Portsmouth—with good results. He's still around, living in Kingston upon Thames. Lonesome Dave is now deceased, and Kim as well. (*Ed. note*: Chris Youlden passed in 2025.)

Dave was not, as I recall, a very outward-going guy, but nor was he a recluse. He was a fine guitarist and no mean vocalist, but I only ever saw him in the studio or onstage. The same could be said of my relationship with Kim. He was a pleasure to work with—as were all Savoy Brown members while I was their producer. Once again, I never really got to know him that well—outside the studio. Kim, with his Flying V guitar, was in full control of his destiny, and over the years he developed a vocal styling that suited his needs. He was a true bluesman, and he will not be forgotten.

Rest in peace, Kim Maiden Simmonds.

# INTRODUCTION

But the twilight faded and then burnt out,
and the day was gone past recalling.
—Bjørnstjerne Björnson

When do all the gigs, the traveling, and the cities and towns start becoming a blur? It doesn't take long before the faces you meet meld into one another, and the gigs become a fog in your memory.

It all began for me, as a performing musician, in 1966 at the Nags Head Pub on York Road in Battersea, South London. I had formed my band, Savoy Brown, in late 1965, and then each week, in the new year, I'd turn up to do a Monday night show. Well, I remember it as a Monday night, but I was reminded recently that, in fact, it was a Wednesday night show (there's my memory going).

My brain would be in a scramble from working all week, and my body would be itching to get onstage to feel the thrill of performing in front of an audience . . . an audience of one's own making. There was no hype or hit records to make anyone show up. Word of mouth got around. Blues fans, starved for new music, were looking for a band playing something fresh, and they would find the venue. It was a great band playing cutting-edge music. That was the reason so many paid at the door. That was why they braved coming to a dingy, run-down, working-class area in an unfashionable part of South London. From a few stragglers to a packed room each week, it grew almost immediately, or so it seemed. From there, it was on to tour throughout the UK, with brother Harry booking the gigs and tour manager Brian leading the way.

Eventually, via America and Europe and far-flung places around the world, the reality of doing hundreds and hundreds of gigs amassed into an impressive career for myself, but I have had to turn a blind eye to the humdrum. How does one do it? I've simply had the patience for it. Whatever you have the patience for in life is likely what you'll succeed at.

Of course, my life started way before Battersea. I was born in Wales, in a small mining town, amid a postwar Britain that was still reeling from the Second World War, which had affected every family. I have survived childhood trauma, dysfunctional early family life, and a life constantly on the move.

From Wales, I moved with my family to London, and it all culminated with my immigration to the United States in 1980. Even then, I kept moving. After initially settling in the Midwest, there was an excursion to Hollywood Hills and the eventual settling down in the central New York area, which has been my happy home for the past thirty-plus years. When all was said and done, I had found myself a few miles from Lake Ontario and thousands of miles from my birth town.

One trait of mine has gotten me through countless angst-filled years, life's rich tapestry, and thousands of band shows—I'm very good at blotting out reality. I think I became very good at forgetting things because I had such good practice, at an early age, of erasing the unsavory memories of my childhood. As someone once said, "Look to the future, that's where you'll be living the rest of your life." I've tried to live my life that way. Whatever the reasons, I have been on the road for six decades. Did I say six decades? Who does the same thing for that long? Not many. Patience!

In the pages you're about to read, you'll find my life story, personal reminisces, road stories, and some humor and soul-searching. The humor is a good way to hide from that pesky thing known as reality. Soul-searching is the hard part, coming to terms with your conscience. There's no hiding from that.

I have crossed paths with many famous celebrities, musicians in particular, from the 1960s and 1970s. From Tom Jones, Rod Stewart, and Jimi Hendrix to Peter Green, Fleetwood Mac, and John Lee Hooker. I have been restless.

I have lived with an inner nervousness that I could harness to make things happen. I could place my will on circumstances and move events to my own liking. Often, that nervousness, the unbridled energy I've been blessed with, has led me into trouble—into bankruptcy, into a hell of my own making, into divorce, and into other estrangements. However, it also gave me a career as a bandleader stretching these long decades. That was worth all the pain. I was born a dreamer, and some say a loner. I have God to thank, first and foremost, for giving me the drive to succeed. I also thank my parents; my inherent DNA; my wife, Debbie; my family; and the support from friends and dozens of musicians who have come and gone in my life.

I have been impetuous. I have been naive. I have lacked common sense. I have acted selfishly. I have played great guitar, mediocre guitar, and sublime poetic guitar. I have let myself be blown about by the four winds. I have been a working professional, but I have not cared about money. I have supported countless musicians. I have let myself and others down. However, I have grown into the person I always wanted to be. It took me years and years, and the support of numerous friends and the love of Debbie, a very special woman, to get me to this place where I can say that I've matured.

I have had countless musicians in my band. Some great, some average, but all have been worthy. Without their collective help, I wouldn't have been able to keep Savoy Brown going as an entity. My career would have stalled in 1967, when I first had to look for musicians to fill vacancies in my band. Very few musicians came knocking on my door. Were there any? I had to go out and find them, either by literally knocking on THEIR door or by holding auditions. The latter situation was often a nightmare of sorting out someone eligible to play in a very scant period of time, usually in an afternoon with lots of people competing for a job. I've given all the musicians a platform to be the best they could be. That is how I've always run the band. I want people to excel so that I can excel, and the band can excel. I have never run the band as a means for me to have power over people or to build myself up. If that did happen, it happened through happenstance.

I've kept myself from getting soft, or losing the fire, by staying in the trenches and playing up close and personal to anybody who would pay for a ticket. I've played a variety of venues since those halcyon days of the 1960s and 1970s . . . theaters, auditoriums, arenas, halls, hockey rinks, and bars. The list goes on and on. I've never been afraid of playing small clubs. A small crowd, with its intimate atmosphere, is where the magic happens.

Yes, it may come with a whole host of logistical problems, and the comfort level can easily be zero. However, I know that has kept me in touch with what I'm all about . . . the music and the fans. It's not about myself. It's always been about the audience and the music.

I've reached the lofty age above the normal three score and ten that had been the lifespan expectation of a man, at least in centuries before. Now, science and medicine have made it possible for us all to live longer if we're lucky or have the right DNA. I feel I've given my life to music and to enriching people's lives through playing my guitar. Does that sound awfully high-toned? Well, let's just say it's been a privilege to have been given all these years of creativity from the most creative force in the world . . . God.

Somerset Maugham said the hardest thing about growing old is the burden of memories. I'll place my memories here for you to engage in, and, maybe, I'll rest my burden for a while.

I hope you enjoy reading this book. Let music make our lives a little sweeter.

# CHAPTER 1

## BEGINNINGS, WALES, AND NEWBRIDGE

Happy the man whose wish and care,
a few paternal acres abound.
—Alexander Pope

I was born in 1947 in Newbridge, Wales, in the county of Monmouthshire, which is now known by its original Welsh name, Gwent. It was a small coal-mining town. The name Newbridge comes from a bridge built across the Ebbw River. I'll never know how many times I risked my young life crawling across the coal mine pipes that spanned the River Ebbw. However, that was the way to the mountains, and a place to play among the tramlines and coal buckets going to the top to spill out their loads of slag.

Newbridge is the English given name. The original Welsh name, Trecelyn ("place of the holly trees"), was long lost by the twentieth century. My mother kept reminding me that the town, by the time I was born, was really in English territory and that I was as much English as I was Welsh. One of my grandfathers was German, so I definitely, like most of us, have mixed blood. There have been times when I've felt Welsh more than anything else; yet, there have been other times when I've noticed the German trait strong within me. The English influence seems to have really overtaken me in many ways. That being said, I'm sure I get my enthusiasm and energy from my Celtic blood.

The most famous building in my hometown was, and still is, the Memo (Memorial Hall). It was built for coal miners in 1925 as a place for entertainment and drinking and also to commemorate the men who never returned from the First World War. It was the place to congregate. It had a beautiful art deco style to it and has now been refurbished. It was built to last, as they say, made of red brick with black, steep-slanted, tiled roofs. I returned and played a solo show there, to help in that cause, in the 1990s. At that time, funds were needed for the refurbishment.

My father, Henry Simmonds, had been a navy man. Everyone called him Harry. He had joined the Royal Navy in the early 1930s to avoid being sent down into the local coal mine by his parents. The mines were where most men worked. Hundreds of black-faced coal miners would walk the streets back to their homes after their shift ended. The pay in the 1950s was good . . . well, it wasn't bad. Coal mining was at its zenith in the 1950s and was the biggest single employer in Wales. However, there was quite a price to pay. Black lung was a dreadful killer of the colliers. We called it black lung, but its true name is anthracosis. Cigarette smoking, which nearly everyone of that generation did, only made matters worse. I saw firsthand the effects of black lung and smoking with my stepgrandfather, Billy Nick . . . coughing and loss of appetite leading to a bad ending. The old Welsh lyric captures the feeling of inevitability the miners must have felt:

It's bread when I'm hungry,
And beer when I'm dry.
It's bed when I'm tired,
And heaven when I die.

My father had a stocky athletic build and stood about 5 foot 8. He had started to lose his hair quite early in life. He blamed it on always having to wear a navy hat since he was sixteen years old. He played rugby for the navy and had an air of confidence and intelligence about him that perhaps came from experience . . . or are we born with those attributes? Later in life, he would never write down telephone numbers or important data like that. He simply memorized everything. It was amazing. In his seventies, he did an inventory of a small local auto supplies store in another town, Tredegar, simply with pencil and paper.

Not only did he have brains, but he was equally skilled when it came to using his hands. He was adept at brickwork, plumbing, and electrical wiring. You name it, and he could do it all. He was a serious man and a conservative in political thought. He never mentioned religion. He was very smart and excelled in school, but his parents wouldn't pay for his further education and expected him to work in the coal mine. He ran away for a life at sea.

My father received his training in Portsmouth, the famous naval base along the southern coast of England. He showed immense promise in winning medals for climbing the rigging and other novice challenges. He was an established navy man when World War II came around, and he would have chosen to be a career man if my mother hadn't given him an ultimatum: "Leave the navy, or I take our son, Henry, and elope with another man." Of course, I am paraphrasing. The other man in question was an American serviceman. My father quit the navy. His superiors tried to make him see things differently . . . he had been an officer with a brilliant future in front of him. He stuck by his decision and returned to Newbridge, Wales, his and our family's hometown. My birth certificate states he was an electrician. I've seen photos of him in that time period, and he seemed happy. However, he wasn't. He had a dark side.

I believe that returning from war and giving up his natural career led my father toward a tendency for hard drinking. He told me later that at sea, around the captain's table, the officers would drink heavily but would be expected not to show it. They'd be drunk as a skunk but acted as if they were totally in control. I guess that's one way to deal with stress. He often found himself on many ships protecting convoys, hunting U-boats, and avoiding the bombs aimed by German planes. Describing the bombs in the sky, he told me, "They looked like the size of houses." He was on the ship's bridge and witnessed how his captain would wait for the right time to steer the ship to port or starboard, and, with luck, the bombs would fall harmlessly into the ocean. One of his captains had to be let off at one port due to stress and nervous exhaustion.

My father had two childhood friends who were twins, and they had joined the navy with him. Sadly, they died at sea in a U-boat attack. The twins had been on a ship my father was supposed to have served on, but he had been called away to London. Later, he visited the twins' parents back in Newbridge to offer his condolences following their deaths. The parents slammed the door in his face, blaming him for leading their sons to their eventual fate.

I believe that the combination of the war experience and my father's sense of underachievement led to his heavy drinking. There were, at times, violent fights between him and my mother. One of my first childhood recollections was one night, sitting on the stairs that led upstairs, looking down along the hallway and out the front door to see my parents physically fighting in the street. I remember my mother seeing me and saying, "Kim's awake." The fighting stopped. At one point, my father, in a presumably drunken rage, destroyed an entire heavy wooden bedroom set with his bare hands. There is more, but it seems churlish to dish dirt on a man who had a marvelous intellect and enormous integrity, and one who has shaped and defined me.

I never really knew my grandparents. My mother had a stepdad who was part of the extended family, as well as a stepsister. However, very little, if anything, was ever spoken about my mother's birth parents. On my dad's side, I have only very sparse memories of those grandparents. I do know they were very wary of electric home lighting, which didn't appear in many Welsh homes until the late 1930s. My father couldn't convince them that it was costing them farthings to run. They still would use only candles and oil lamps at night when I visited them with my parents. That lifestyle was repeated on other visits we made to friends with farms in the area. Even in the early 1950s, people in rural areas of Wales still used oil lamps and candles for lighting.

My mother, Phylis, was a small-town girl, very attractive, and loved to dance. Her hair was fine, and her complexion was clean. There was a rose tint to her cheeks, and she cooked very well. She was not good at housecleaning, but the house was always decently cared for. She loved the sound of the harmonica. She loved me, and, perhaps, I was her favorite between my brother and myself. At least, I was "little Kim," and my older brother was expected to look after me. Who knew that expectation would continue until I was thirty years of age? My mother had a neurotic side that I now recognize in myself . . . we do turn into our parents, of course. For years, I thought I had taken after my mother. However, when I was beyond fifty, my sister-in-law Olwen and other family members were shocked when they realized how much I then looked like my father.

I loved my parents, and I know they loved me, but not once in my life do I recall any of us saying, "I love you" to each other. Those were the days, at least in Britain, when the sentiment was accepted but didn't need to be said. I was always aware of my mother wanting to pamper me. I was certainly spoiled as a child and developed what now could be considered anorexia. I simply would not eat. Eventually, the doctor told my mother to leave bread, butter, and jam on the table.

"Let him go and make a sandwich himself if he wants" was the doctor's advice.

I did make my own sandwiches, and, to this day, my favorite food is a jam sandwich. However, I am now thoroughly Americanized, and I add peanut butter and bananas (I always wanted to be Elvis). The only problem was I never regained a full appetite until I reached my thirties. For instance, as a boy, I could eat only half an apple. Therefore, I never did get above 112 pounds in weight until my late thirties. It made for a good "look" when I finally became a musician on the stage . . . rail thin like a female model. In addition, with the name Kim, I fit the moving androgynous times perfectly.

I did spend a lot of time in the hospital during childhood . . . at one point at death's door. My memories of that are having to take extremely hot baths to help heal me after operations, and the nurses getting frustrated with me because the heat was too much. The bed was very high off the floor. I tumbled out of that a number of times in the middle of the night. I guess that was before they invented bedside bars.

Growing up, I was also acutely shy, and it was a problem. I overheard my father tell my mother, "He'll grow out of it," but I never really did. What I DID do was try to camouflage my shyness. My personality can make me look as if I'm in control and cool, especially onstage, but inside, I'm a basket case. It probably led me to become a bit of a loner and to stay in my own thoughts. It often prevented me from joining in with the crowd and making friends. Sometimes, I'd have to be dragged along to the party, which, inevitably, I would enjoy. In adulthood, I'd use alcohol to break down my barriers, and that worked fine. I could be a different and gregarious person when drinking, but that dependency was also a sign of trouble ahead.

My mother was philosophical while my dad was practical. In those regards, I am more like my mother and less like my dad. I did have artistic talent, and that had been made apparent to me by my mother. She made me take piano lessons and took me to elocution lessons (perhaps with acting in mind) in an attempt to bring my imagined talent forward. The speech lessons were fun, and the teacher would have me memorize "The Owl and the Pussycat" until I could say it in perfect intonation, speaking every vowel and consonant clearly and precisely.

Mom gave me the general impression that I was meant to be "somebody." She always pointed to my thin, spindly fingers and said, "You're going to be an artist." She kept a book of cuttings of collected philosophical writings, and she had a hidden streak of artiness about her. She imparted all of that to me. She wanted me to be different and not part of the crowd. As a result, I wasn't allowed to play on the streets with the other kids. There's something to be said for that approach, although I hated it at the time. She was a stay-at-home mom, as most were in those days, so she had time to devote to me and spoil me. She instilled in me the feeling that I should be an artist.

Our first house in Newbridge was a row house on a steep hill on Penarth Street. All the houses were built for the coal miners and had 2-foot-thick walls constructed of the same natural mountain stone. Nowadays, there are no coal mines. The slag heaps have been manicured over, and the only remnant of coal mining is the Big Pit, the mine museum.

The thick stone kept the houses warm in the winter and cool in the summer months. On Penarth Street, none of the houses had a bathroom, and the outside toilet was found at the back of the yard. Everyone bathed in an aluminum tub. I'm certain my first baths were in that fashion, but we very soon had the first house on the street with a modern bathroom and indoor toilet attached . . . built by my dad.

We moved a few times within the town. Each time, my parents would buy a DIY house project. My dad would do the work and sell the beautified house at a profit. One of these houses was just around the corner from the Newbridge Hotel, itself a beautiful late Victorian stone building that had been built in 1898.

At night, I'd go on walks with my mother and father. We had no television for the first ten years of my life. Those walks were our entertainment. I was a dreamer. During those walks, my mind would wander far and wide over the Welsh hills to remote parts of the world I had only read about in fairy tales . . . stories of secret woods and meadows and dangerous wild animals to fight off. My mind was always working, dreaming . . . imagining.

One night, with my head in the clouds, I was brought swiftly back to Earth when, as we walked along a dimly lit street, I walked straight into a lamppost! I rubbed the side of my head, and we carried on walking. Lesson learned.

I learned to ride my bicycle at this time. My dad would hold the rear seat from behind and act as a stabilizer as I slowly pedaled. One day, I looked behind and realized he wasn't holding the seat, and I had been merrily pedaling without support. Of course, at that point, I immediately tumbled in a heap to the ground, followed by my bike. From then on, I could ride my bike alone, and, in many ways, that has been a metaphor for my whole life.

Then came the upheaval that saw me taken from the Welsh mountains and valleys to the smoke-and-smog-filled world of 1950s London.

# CHAPTER 2

## BROTHER HARRY, FIRST MUSICAL EXPERIENCES, MOVING TO LONDON, AND MY "REAL" NAME

Art is the most intense mode of individualism that the world has known.

—Oscar Wilde

My older brother was named after my father, Henry Simmonds, and also came to be known as Harry later in life. Harry, as I shall call him, had conditioned my mind in music since he bought his first record in 1953. That was "Cry" by Johnnie Ray. He played that 78 rpm record continually, and I was part of the captive audience. Harry also had a Mario Lanza record that he had been given for Christmas. He wasn't keen on that one, and I quickly learned from those two recordings that there was music with an edge and music that was more conventional.

From that point on, I tagged along behind my older brother throughout the 1950s as he discovered rock and roll, blues, and jazz. Together, we saw the movie *Rock Around the Clock*, which featured Bill Haley & His Comets. Harry was a member of the Haley Fan Club. For me, Haley's first album is still a good example of how to record in the studio. At least, it's how I still often record—everyone playing live with no overdubs.

Harry sported an Elvis Presley–styled haircut with a large quiff, and he poured on plenty of Brylcreem. He was always in an energetic and excited mood, and he could tell a great story. I imagine that today he would be considered to have ADHD. His enthusiasm was guaranteed to keep you enthralled when he spoke about things that interested him . . . music, books, and movies. I would be captivated when he would tell me about a movie he had just seen, or listen to his critique of a musical artist. He had blue eyes that shone like the Brylcreem on his hair. Although he hadn't a body full of muscles, his lean frame looked solid as a rock. He laughed a lot. I was his kid brother. I'd always be his kid brother, but he had great respect for my talent when it flowered.

We went to see the movie *Blackboard Jungle*, featuring the Bill Haley song "Rock Around the Clock," as well as the movies *Don't Knock the Rock* and *Rock, Rock, Rock!* The artist who performed the title track song on the latter movie was Jimmy Cavallo with his band, the House Rockers. I must have been eight years old. Amazingly, when Jimmy was in his eighties, he recorded in my home studio, and the record went on to be nominated for a Grammy Award. It turned out that Cavallo had roots not far from me in Syracuse, New York, and was recording for Blue Wave Records, owned by Greg Spencer.

Greg and I were friends and had worked together. He was the first to see the possibilities of my studio, and he did a great job producing the record. I was the engineer for the sessions, a first for me. I felt relaxed and enjoyed my behind-the-scenes role. You can do no wrong when a great artist like Jimmy Cavallo steps in front of a microphone. He was one of the first great, white rhythm-and-blues singers, and he also played a superb saxophone.

It was hard for me to believe that the man I had seen at the movie house in a small town in Wales back in 1956 was in my studio, decades later, blowing his sax and singing up a storm.

In those aforementioned movies, I also saw Little Richard, who became a favorite of mine. I'd play my brother's Little Richard 78s constantly. I loved the drums on those recordings and later found out it was Earl Palmer. Earl was, to my mind, the drummer who invented the modern rock-and-roll style. Fats Domino was another favorite of mine. The song "The Fat Man" was recorded by Fats in 1949. It is, arguably, the first rock-and-roll record. Who was the drummer? None other than Earl Palmer! Palmer should be lionized in the world of music above all other drummers. However, I speak for myself in that regard.

Harry held a pivotal place in my life. Since he was seven years older than me, there was almost a generational gap between us. He had my father's quick mind and memory. He put the latter to such good use. He once memorized a complete school task and was accused of cheating on a test by the masters because they believed that no one could know all that he knew! As a result of the incident, my dad was called into school, and there was a huge confrontation. I also remember an incident in which my brother nearly lost an eye to an arrow. Young boys made their own bows and arrows in those days . . . and they were for real. My brother seemed larger than life to me. I'm sure he resented me as the young one in the family, because I got more attention. Isn't that how it always seems to go? Once he played a prank on me by balancing pepper on a door jamb. When I opened the door, I got a peppered face, which was not much fun. My mother dusted Harry down for that. It was a mean thing to do but, in general, we got along.

Harry rebelled at the age of fifteen and went to work in the local coal mine. My parents were aghast. However, there was money to be made in the mines, and the coal-mining life was all around us. It was an easy influence. I often saw those black-faced coal miners walk up our street at the end of a shift. My grandfathers had been coal miners. Everyone, it seemed, worked in the collieries. I played on the slag heaps with my friends. The coal dust was always in the air and mixed with a constant fine rain drizzle from the clouds as they swept over the steep mountains around us.

An enduring memory of mine is listening to my brother's stories when he returned from working the mines each day. He could dramatize, that's for sure, and I was enthralled by tales of the heroes he met working in the dark . . . "on hands and knees digging for coal." Harry worked the coal face with an undercutting machine. After the coal was cut, he would put it on a conveyor belt by hand. Often, a shovel was the "machine." The roofs were held up by wooden pit props, and there were canaries in cages to signal gas leaks.

Eventually, my father got fed up with life and his relative failure in Newbridge and left the family for London. Naval friends of his had pulled some strings, and he found a job in the Foreign Office. There was another woman involved in this move, but he did give my mother the option to join him. When my mother did join him, the other woman disappeared, and we carried on as a family unit. We lived initially in a flat in Bayswater in central London. Bayswater, even then, was a very cosmopolitan area. It was no surprise that the flat was above an Indian restaurant, and we'd often eat dinner there. The owners and cooks were so friendly, and the food was delicious. Turmeric, cumin, and cinnamon mixed with fennel. Such aromas! The chicken was slow-cooked in ovens. That started my love of cooking Indian cuisine, and nowadays my specialty is a chicken curry made from scratch. That is to say, starting first by grinding my own fresh spices. My house often smells like that Bayswater restaurant from so long ago. It was, though, a lonely time spent mostly with my mother within the confines of a couple of furnished rooms. I can't remember any conversations, and I guess it must have been during the summer months, because I didn't go to school.

After living in a second furnished flat in South London, my parents eventually bought a detached house in the London suburb of Crystal Palace. Again, it was another dilapidated home eventually made wonderful by my dad's "do it yourself" skills and hard work. It was quite an impressive house. There were large bay windows on either side of a large, central oak front door. My dad converted the upstairs into a separate living space, and it was rented out. As usual, we lived in the kitchen and living room at the back of the house. The front sitting room, with the best furniture, was kept as a place to entertain visitors . . . which we never had. The house had no central heating . . . hardly any houses had that luxury. It was, inevitably, cold and damp because of the climate. Stand-alone electric fires, with two or three heating bars, in addition to the occasional coal fire, kept us warm. A coal fire was not as common, since it was simply easier to plug in a heater. At bedtime, we would fill up plastic hot-water bottles and heat up the beds before retiring. Temperatures generally stayed no lower than the 40s, so it wasn't freezing, but those beds certainly still felt cold even with a hot-water bottle.

There was a huge garden and a separate garage at the back of the property. The house had painted white stone walls with gloss black window surrounds. That was my dad's favorite way of painting the outside of a house. He'd always say that white and black is the best, simplest, and classiest way of decorating the outside of the house. Guess what color scheme my New York house has?

Crystal Palace had its own great history. It was famous for its mammoth cast-iron-and-plate-glass architectural marvel called the Crystal Palace, which was part of the World's Fair Expo of 1851. Unfortunately, the building burned down in the 1930s. The area is in South London and got its name from that exhibition building. In the nineteenth century, the area included many acres of woodland . . . the Great North Wood was a natural oak forest that had covered much of the area south of central London. The forest had been home to gypsies, so living where we were may have been a good place for me. I, myself, was soon to become a gypsy of sorts. Interestingly, one of my favorite impressionist painters, Camille Pissarro, stayed in Crystal Palace and painted the area in 1871. I have a copy of one of those paintings on my wall today. From the time we moved to Crystal Palace, until I was thirty years of age, I was a South London person. It got into my blood.

In those days, we didn't have a television, and I'd have to go to a school friend's house to watch programs such as *The Cisco Kid* and Roger Moore starring in *Ivanhoe*. Moore became a hero of mine and remained so throughout his time as James Bond. School was within walking distance, perhaps a mile or so, and I made friends easily in the neighborhood. We'd walk to school in all types of weather. If it thundered, with lightning and rain, we'd simply shelter under one of the many trees that lined the suburban streets.

It was as if a magic wand had been waved when I found myself in the Crystal Palace home. Even the name of that London area sounds magical now. It was the late 1950s, and the family consisted of my father, mother, and brother and my brother's Welsh girlfriend, Olwen. Olwen was allowed to come and live with us to pacify my brother and to make the move from Wales a comfortable experience for him. They would eventually marry, divorce, and marry again. However, that would be much later. Olwen was a steadying influence on my brother and the whole family. She had short hair and a round face. Her pleasantness was plain to see, and she always treated me wonderfully. She was hardworking, always employed, and not a flighty person. We had never taken a family vacation until she came to live at the house. It was through her encouragement that we ended up renting caravans at vacation beaches and having fun in the sand. Cockles were a family favorite, and, on vacation, we would find our own in the rocks by the sea. We'd cook them up and have a great dinner time.

Life was good in other ways in Crystal Palace. I saw my first football/soccer match when the local team played Arsenal. Mel Charles, the great Welsh international, played center forward for that team. I sat on my father's shoulders.

My brother tried to become a policeman but failed out of the academy . . . the rumor was because of health, but I think there was more to it. I'll never know what the "more" could have been.

I was happy watching old movies on the television we eventually bought. I also enjoyed playing the triangle in the school band. I also had a part in a school play. All I had to do was frown a lot in my role, but I found that hard to do since I was so content. I always had a smile on my face. From that first stage performance, it was obvious that I wasn't going to be an actor, although, in the band, I did well with the triangle!

The dark side of my father's life faded somewhat. Very often, in the summer and winter, he would take me walking after coming home from work in the evening. The destination was a railway station bar where he could drink. There was a bench seat outside for me to have my lemonade. The night air always felt great, and I enjoyed the walks even if nothing was said. In fact, usually, nothing was said. Yes, it was as it sounds . . . melancholic. After a while, sitting outside with my lemonade, I'd start to feel uncomfortable. I could see my dad at the bar drinking alone. Eventually, to my relief, he'd come out and we'd return home. We held hands and that was that.

On a happier note, this is the time I put together my first band. I brought together my neighborhood friends in the loft of our garage and assembled them along with various cardboard boxes and cans. I gave everyone roles to play, and I was to be the singer. They banged away on the boxes, in rhythm or out of rhythm, and I sang an Elvis Presley song. There you have it. Little did I know that my fate was to be a bandleader for practically the rest of my life.

It was during this time that the threat of nuclear war always loomed on the horizon. I was aware of this by watching the news at night and seeing the "Ban the bomb" protest marches. Russia was the enemy, although my dad always warned me about the militant, terrorist Muslims. He was somewhat clairvoyant in that regard.

I had only casual friends during this time period, and I can't remember having a best friend. Best friends have been hard to come by all through my life. Of course, we always moved so much, and it was difficult to keep friends. The move to London was especially uprooting. I've continued that model through much of my life, continually moving while in the UK and also after immigrating to the United States in 1980 . . . finally settling in the most unlikely place of snowbound central New York. At least, I've stayed here for the past quarter of a century and more.

Before I leave this chapter, I should elaborate on the tease at the beginning regarding my real name. It starts with my father . . . doesn't everything? My father was born out of wedlock, and to avoid social disgrace he was given to Sarah, who was married. She pretended that my father was her son, and he was reared as a Simmonds (Sarah was married to Dai Simmonds). My father's true mother married Arthur Ackerman, the man who had gotten her pregnant. Arthur was a German Jew who came to Wales to mine coal. He was renowned in our valley as a strong, strong individual. The Ackerman family lived nearby.

No one knew the truth about my father's birth situation, although there always seemed to be something dubious about this in the air as I grew up. The truth finally came out when my father was in his sixties and retiring. There was no record of there being a Henry Simmonds in certain places!

He discovered that Dai Simmonds had let Arthur Ackerman officially claim him back, as his son, without telling Sarah or anyone else. So, my dad was officially Henry Ackerman, and thus, in some way, I am Kim Ackerman! Of course, things didn't turn out that way, and I am a Simmonds on my birth certificate. We were all old enough to laugh about it when the true story was revealed, and my father straightened out any inconsistencies in the official paperwork. However, I don't think Sarah Simmonds would have found it funny at all . . . a child she had brought up as her own was signed away by her secretive husband.

So now I move on with my story, along with that blood mixture of Welsh, English, and German.

# CHAPTER 3

## WANDSWORTH, SCHOOL, AND I SEE THE LIGHT

Beauty depends on simplicity.
—Plato

After moving from Wales to London in the late 1950s, I was caught in the exciting new rock-and-roll music scene. My first exposure to these new British music trends was on two weekly TV series, *Oh Boy!* and *Boy Meets Girls*. Joe Brown was a featured artist on *Boy Meets Girls*, and he was a very good rock guitarist. I liked watching and listening to him. His playing caught my ear, and I liked the look of his guitar, which I believe was a Gibson 335 model. Lord Rockingham's X1 was the house band on *Oh Boy!*, and organist Cherry Wainer was a standout entertainer with the band. Band member Red Price also rocked out on the saxophone. Both of those TV shows, produced by Jack Good, were exciting productions and featured all the rock-and-roll artists who were prominent or just starting their careers in the UK at the time. I was more interested in the guitar sounds than I was the front-man singers such as Cliff Richard, Marty Wilde, and Billy Fury. Vic Flick (he played the original James Bond theme) was another guitarist who got my imagination working and thinking that I could play guitar. I saw Vic playing an early guitar instrumental, with the John Barry Seven, called "Hit and Miss." The song was a chart hit in 1960 and even featured a guitar solo, which seemed a rarity to me at the time. Flick played a Gibson 175D model guitar in the Duane Eddy style for that recording, and I later saw him playing a Fender Telecaster. He looked like a serious and professional musician, and that quality attracted me.

Selling our detached house in Crystal Palace, the family moved into a terraced house on Marcilly Road in Wandsworth, South West London, so my father could be closer to work. Gout was beginning to be a problem for him. From Wandsworth, a train ride from Clapham Junction (a train station within walking distance) or a bus ride could get you to the heart of the city in thirty minutes. It was about 4 miles from the center of London. Again, it was a case of buying a house needing repairs on a less-than-glamorous street. We moved in as the floorboards were being replaced . . . by my dad. At the time, I thought that this move to a small row house, from a nice, detached home, was a step down in status. However, these days, a million pounds could just about purchase a row house like that.

It was a quiet neighborhood, and I could walk to my school in about twenty minutes or so. The street led to Wandsworth Common, a large green park bordered by chestnut trees. That's where I spent many an hour playing soccer after school and collecting chestnuts. We'd have competitions with the chestnuts, and we called them conkers. As schoolboys, we would tie one end of a length of string through the chestnut and hold on to the other end of the string, leaving the chestnut to dangle. Then, two boys would take turns striking each other's conker until one broke. It was great fun. I'd soak my conker in vinegar in an attempt to make it harder to survive more games.

After the Marcilly house was made shipshape by my dad's handiwork, the decorating began. Wallpaper was always the wall covering of choice in all the family homes I lived in. Of course, in my family, nothing was easy.

One time, my father had spent quite some time papering one room to perfection with a professional look. My mother decided she didn't like it . . . off the paper came, and he repapered the room. Oh yes, there was a lot of huffing and puffing in addition to some choice words over that episode.

My father's gout became less of a problem, but the time he spent away from home on foreign assignments for the Foreign Office did become a problem. He would be sent to trouble spots in the world, undercover in Africa, for instance, as part of an intelligence team. He might also get plum postings to countries such as Greece. I once saw him leave with no baggage, but only a toothbrush poking from his suit pocket. These trips could last a few months. My mother found herself back in a familiar position . . . alone.

Maybe that's what all their fighting was about. My dad certainly didn't avoid the ladies on those jaunts away. I would find that out much later. When he returned from those trips, he always arrived carrying presents. Now, that was the fun part. My mother was never happy with her presents. I guess nothing could make up for his deserting her. Eventually, the foreign trips ended, and life settled down.

Moving to South West London coincided with my next phase of schooling. I had failed the eleven-plus. The eleven-plus was a standardized examination used to determine which type of school a student should go to after the age of eleven. According to how well you did on the test, you were either streamed into grammar school, secondary modern school, or a technical school. My failure meant I was bound for secondary school. I ended up going to the Spencer Park Comprehensive School. It was a school of about twelve hundred pupils that was a mixture of grammar-school types, secondary pupils, and technical boys. It really was a good school, with a chapel, an outdoor swimming pool, an old Victorian section, and a brand-new building. I started my first year in the old building, where only the ground floor could be used (the upper floors were rotting away). I was in the new building for my second year onward. There were A to F grade levels according to your academic ability. I started in 1C and progressed to the A grade in my third year. My parents couldn't afford the top-line school uniform. I ended up with the coarser woolen blazers (of course, initially with short trousers and then graduating to long slacks).

Many might not be able to relate to my school experience. It was the era of the cane in British schools . . . corporal punishment for being a bad boy. The cane was used across your hand in class or on the backside as delivered by the headmaster. I was on the receiving end a couple of times in class for being cheeky, especially in the French language class. "Seemonds," my French teacher would say, "Seemonds, come to the front of the class."

I'd then receive a swipe or two across my open palm. The internet tells me that corporal punishment lasted, at least in theory, I imagine, until 1987. That amazes me. For me, it was Dickensian in 1960!

Once May came around, the unheated swimming pool came into use during physical education classes. The brave boys would jump right in, while the rest of us would be freezing around the pool until the master smacked our backsides with his plimsoll and off we went.

Now, this swimming pool was the location of my first "religious experience" . . . or was it a near-death experience? Or was it both or was it neither? Let me explain. One day, I was freezing in the pool. I had already been coaxed into the water. Next to me in the pool, I remember, was a fellow pupil with incredibly white skin. He could not be touched due to the possibility of instant bruising, which I now realize was probably hemophilia or some other bleeding disorder. We both were shivering in the shallow end and held our arms around our upper bodies. I wanted to ask him if he was okay but thought better of it. Kids that were out of the ordinary were usually given a wide berth by everyone. I, too, at the time, didn't understand his situation and watched him from a distance. It was so cold this one day that I felt I had to move in some way to keep my mind off how I felt. I moved slowly into the deep end, clinging to the side, but I couldn't swim. Why I moved to the deep end and just didn't splash in my own shallow area I don't know. There were kids having a great time jumping off the diving board. I saw my pal Andrew jumping and splashing as if it was summer and we were at the seaside. I closed my eyes as the chlorine in the water stung my eyes. I lost my grip. I sank once and thrashed around. I sank twice and flailed for my life. I sank a third time, and suddenly it seemed I was in heaven. A beautiful peace came over me, and there, in front of me, appeared a beautiful bright light. I started to move toward the light when I suddenly found myself pulled headfirst from the water. I was saved, but by whom I don't know. Did that someone even realize I was drowning? Had it been Andrew? To this day, I don't know. I simply got on my feet and acted as if nothing had happened. I told no one about the experience. I doubted it myself. I pretended nothing had happened. I was also embarrassed.

"What an idiot," I thought to myself. The feeling of contentment, the looking at the bright light, and the beckoning feeling were all then pushed to the back of my mind, like so many things I had artfully managed to do in my life. Nowadays, they say that experience happens because of a lack of oxygen to the brain. That's a good scientific explanation. All I know is that drowning, at least for me, was going to be an entrance into heaven. I've never been afraid of drowning again. In many ways, I'm unafraid of dying.

There were many lighter moments. I joined the school summer excursions every year. Two wonderful experiences were trips to the Isles of Scilly and to the Peak District National Park in Derbyshire. I was born with a desire to travel. The trip to Derbyshire was by train, and I loved sitting in a compartment watching the landscape sweep by me. We stayed at the YMCA in the market town of Matlock. From there, we would climb the nearby hills with our teacher, exploring the land, before having cheese sandwiches and crusty bread for lunch. The town was dead at night, and there was little trouble to get into. A local policeman patrolled on foot and kept a watchful eye on us fourteen-year-olds as we hung around the vending machines that sold chocolates and cigarettes. On one of those summer days, while climbing a rugged hill, we stopped for a break. I was some distance away from the rest of the group with my good friend, Chris Standen. We figured this was the time I would try smoking a cigarette. Chris had a pack of five Woodbines, and it was exciting to fire up a cigarette and think you were living dangerously. I took a big drag of the fag, as we then called them, and was immediately lightheaded. My first taste of tobacco did not sit well, and that was enough for me. I felt sick to my stomach. A feeling of seasickness came over me. I decided it was not for me, but Chris took to it well. I often wondered what part smoking played in Chris's early demise in his fifties.

It was a boat trip to and from the Scilly Isles. The crossing was fine, and the island was much anticipated. I remember a beautiful day and the island being a peaceful and quiet place. My vivid memory of the excursion is of the return trip to the mainland. The weather was bad, very bad, and the boat was tossed around like a tin can. It was the only time I'd ever been seasick. It was awful, like having the flu. I lay down and felt like vomiting the whole trip home.

In my first year attending Spencer Park, I was participating in my first physical education class. The teacher called out, "Anyone Welsh here in class?"

I put up my hand, "Yes, sir. Here, sir."

"Great!" he shouted, "You're on the rugby team."

I had never played rugby, but it was the Welsh national sport, and my dad had been an excellent player. I went along with the plan, hoping I had inherited some of my dad's talent. Rugby is played in the colder months. I found myself running on a field, wearing shorts and a long rugby shirt, under bracing conditions while eating slices of orange at halftime and changing on the side of the pitch. All the opposing teams seemed much older, taller, and fitter. I was really too small for rugby, but it was supposed to be in my blood, and I gave it a good try. The other players had great fun jumping on me with bone-crushing tackles. No, it didn't pan out.

Bullying at school was always an undercurrent. The regular fights between boys were often vicious. I kept a low profile and had a tough Irish friend, Andrew Curran, who gave me some cover when needed.

By the time I was fifteen, disillusionment with school had set in. It felt like I was being groomed to work in a bank, and that didn't appeal to me at all. I became unruly and spoke back to my teachers. One day, I said to my form master, Mr. Bott, that I didn't want to end up in a dead-end job as he had. I was ashamed as soon as the words came out of my mouth. Mr. Bott smiled and didn't reply. I had been a jerk.

The fights reemerged between my parents, and I'd try to get to sleep upstairs amid dreadful rows going on beneath me. I shared a bedroom with my brother, and Olwen was in her own room. We never spoke of the arguments we heard. I was a happy boy until that period. I distinctly remember asking myself, "How can I be happy when my parents are so troubled?"

Until that point, soccer played a large part in my growing up. After school, I would kick a ball around on Wandsworth Common for hours. I never had the physique to have an athletic career with any of my skills, such as they were. It was up to local teenagers in my group, such as Les Barrett, to hit the big time with professional teams. In his case, that meant playing for our local club, Fulham FC. I still have the desire to be an athlete. I watch and like all sorts of sports. I guess you always want what you can't have. I'd go and watch the local teams. I'd alternate, week to week, seeing Fulham FC and Chelsea FC play. Tickets were cheap, and I'd stand behind the goal to watch Jimmy Greaves and other stars play. Johnny Haynes was my favorite. He was a Fulham player of great skill, and the player who first broke the pay barrier by earning a hundred pounds a week . . . a lot of money at the time.

London, in the early 1960s, was a wonderful city to live in. It had one foot in the past and one foot in the future. The 1940s still hung in the air, with the still-unclaimed and bombed-out buildings from World War II. There were lots of unreal-looking, scarred walls that made it seem like a film set. Old-timers, with flat cloth hats, walked around looking like ghosts from 1920. Average hotel rooms still hadn't been upgraded to include a bath . . . there was only one on every floor. I'd walk everywhere, and when that was not possible, a bus ride or train would take me farther afield. London was quite safe, and I never fell afoul of any "yobs" (the prevailing name for hooligans in those days). My school grades were satisfactory, though my indifference precipitated a falling off as I became more disillusioned with my academic future. I didn't want to work in a bank or behind a desk. I had a couple of school friends, and I'd spent the summer with one going to the museums in London. I did that partly to get some culture and also to chat up the "birds" in the galleries.

I have to credit my English classes for starting my lifelong passion for reading in my early teens. One year, in class, we dissected *Brighton Rock* by Graham Greene, and since then, Greene has become my favorite author. I have collected all his books, read them with joy, and still read them. The *Maigret* series of detective books, written by Georges Simenon, also became a favorite of mine, and I have been addicted to detective and mystery novels ever since. I believe that Edgar Allan Poe was the first to write a detective story. I also read Poe, although the prose was a little ponderous for me. I much preferred the direct and simple structure of Greene's writing. Simplicity, in fact, has been my guiding mantra throughout life. Unfortunately, my life has been anything but simple.

Picasso was the artist I admired most. I was a thorough modernist. *Head of a Woman in a Hat* was a series of paintings he did at the time that I enjoyed looking at art. The art museums always had something of that fashion for me to see.

The first James Bond movie was released in 1962, and I saw it at the Granada in Clapham Junction. The movie made me feel exhilarated, and I felt as if I was walking 6 feet off the ground as I walked home after seeing it. A similar feeling would often return when I played at the Fillmore East, on many occasions, a few years later.

Music was taking a major foothold in my life. It was the beginning of the 1960s, and R&B music started to show in popular hits such as "Hey Baby" by Bruce Channel, and Dion was singing about "Runaround Sue." There were also plenty of novelty hits on the charts, but even those were built around a blues progression. The new pop music was very popular at school, and I joined in with everyone as we tried to sing the hits of the day.

On the other hand, I was also avidly listening to my brother's record collection, including Elmore James songs such as "Dust My Broom" and

"Can't Hold Out." Brother Harry hung out with a new group of guys who had just formed a band and were calling themselves the Rolling Stones. There was an underground rhythm-and-blues scene starting in the clubs pioneered by Alexis Korner, Long John Baldry, and Cyril Davies. I was reading about it, and my brother was telling me about it. I bought records by American blues artists such as Muddy Waters and Howlin' Wolf, the latter being my favorite. I listened to the best blues guitarists on record. The American blues artists seemed like distant gods to me: B.B. King, Freddie King, Earl Hooker, Matt Murphy, and Billy Butler from Bill Doggett's band. I listened to everything I could get my hands on, and I sorted out what appealed to me the most and what I could set aside.

Then, the Beatles came along. I saw them on TV, perhaps their first appearance, playing the first release, "Love Me Do." It sounded similar to the blues records I had been listening to, and the band looked honest and unpretentious. Those were the qualities in the blues music I loved so much. Beatlemania took over the country in 1963, and the band was inspiring every time I saw them on TV. I loved them, even though I wasn't buying their records. They were the first rock band, and I'm sure, without them, I wouldn't have formed Savoy Brown. Eventually, I did buy a Beatles EP that had a cover of a Little Richard song. It was brilliant. An English band was finally matching the American bands I had been listening to in sound and talent.

The Rolling Stones released "Come On," their first single, in 1963. I also bought that but didn't think the sound was as good as any of the American records I had. I went to see the band on their first national tour but was underwhelmed. However, I was still a fan because of Brian Jones. I could tell he was a bluesman, and he played slide guitar really well.

Rhythm and blues was the happening music in London and very quickly took over the whole country. The Kinks were playing Slim Harpo songs. Cliff Bennett was rocking with his band, the Rebel Rousers. John Mayall was around, as was Long John Baldry. Every band had blues harmonica featured in their songs . . . including the Beatles. I knew where the music came from. My brother had the original records; I had been listening to those records since I was twelve years old. I understood what was going on. I had been practicing my guitar playing and copying solos from those records. I knew exactly what rhythm and blues was, and I wanted to be a part of it.

I started going with Harry to see rock-and-roll package shows in 1962 and 1963. The Rolling Stones were on the bill on one of those tours headlined by the Everly Brothers and Bo Diddley. It was the Stones' first tour. Another one of those tours was headlined by Jerry Lee Lewis. He had recently married his young cousin, and that had brought great controversy into his career. However, he brought her out and introduced her onstage. People had accepted the situation by then and applauded them as a couple. There were other package tours . . . one with Little Richard as the star and another with Fats Domino headlining. Of all the shows I've ever seen, the Jerry Lee Lewis performance stands out as one of the two most exciting rock shows I've ever seen, the other being a show when I was on the bill with the Who in England. I thought Pete Townshend had the same energy as Jerry Lee Lewis. That show was in 1969 . . . my favorite year.

# CHAPTER 4

## FIRST GUITAR, AN AUDITION, FIRST GIRLFRIEND, AND THE REAL WORLD

April is the cruelest month,
breeding lilacs out of the dead land.
—T. S. Eliot

The Shadows were THE big guitar band when I was a schoolboy. The guitarist in the band, Hank Marvin, really blazed a trail for all of us who later followed. They were always on television, either backing up Cliff Richards or on their own. The bass player, Jet Harris, had an edge to him . . . that was about it. Otherwise, the music and the band were not at all threatening. In addition, Cliff Richards was musically anemic. I plugged in to be part of the crowd and went to see the hit movie *Summer Holiday* starring Cliff and the Shadows. I also listened to the Shadows' LPs with a friend in the area. There were certain twelve-bar tunes I liked . . . the blues format helped. Everyone around me really liked the Shadows, but I was into Chuck Berry and didn't think the pretty melodies of the Shadows' instrumental music matched up to the American rock and roll I was listening to. Likewise, with Bob Dylan, I couldn't understand how my friends could accept Dylan's harmonica playing and singing when Little Walter was still alive and playing on planet Earth, or the voice of Howlin' Wolf was available to appreciate. I've since come to respect both the Shadows and Bob Dylan enormously. Nowadays, I have large and nostalgic leanings toward the Shadows when I listen to those old hits, and I have many Bob Dylan albums. However, at the time, I was at odds with my fellow young teenagers. I was more into far-edgier music. Little Richard, Elvis, and Chuck Berry were my guys.

During this time, I was doing well at school, especially in the Art and English Departments. Everything came naturally to me. I painted well, I wrote stories well, and I sculpted well. However, in all those endeavors, I was oblivious to technique and simply went with my gut feeling. For instance, my art teacher became exasperated with me when I couldn't explain how I had gotten a painting composition so right. It just came naturally. I had no idea what I was doing. Writer, painter, sculptor? One always wonders what could have been, but I decided I'd like to play guitar. I think that was the result of listening to my brother's records and watching performers on television and in movies.

My decision led to some obvious early questions. How does one play guitar and where does one get a guitar? I was thirteen years old and had saved up some money from a paper round. One day, I saw an ad for a mail-order guitar in the back of my parents' crossword puzzle book. The ad was right next to a Charles Atlas ad that promised muscles the size of a mountain if you'd just send six shillings! I, of course, wanted the guitar, and my interest was also perked up by the selling point that suggested it would help me "make friends at school." I bought a postal money order and sent my hard-earned money to an address somewhere far away. I didn't tell anyone in my family, and the waiting began.

Nothing happened for weeks. I eventually figured I was the victim of a scam. Then one day, lo and behold, from an upstairs window, I saw the postman walking down the street carrying a large box. I knew it was my guitar. I ran downstairs, met the postman at the front door, and took the package to my bedroom. I very excitedly tore open the box. To my surprise, I found out the manufacturers had failed to tell me the guitar would be shipped . . . unassembled! It was an acoustic guitar likely made of the cheapest balsa wood, but there were instructions and the glue was included. I had just put together a Japanese transistor radio (a similar mail-order enterprise), so I was undaunted by the proposition of assembling the guitar.

Now it all gets hazy. I got the strings attached but did not know how to tune it. My life revolved around a small neighborhood area and didn't extend to a wider world. I found a local man who knew something about guitars, and he tuned the instrument for me. I recall him testing the harmonics and noticed that the tips of his fingers were missing. Yes, I find it strange how one can remember small details of the past and yet forget the big picture. I bought myself a cheap, learn-to-play-guitar book. It had been written in the 1940s and had classical guitar as the focus. Following the first pages, I used a footstool, placed my left foot on it, sat my guitar on my raised thigh, and tried placing my fingers in the required barre chord (where the thumb is placed behind the fretboard, and each of the fingers covers a note position). For me, it was an impossible task. There was no way I could even get my palm into the required position around the fretboard. So, I couldn't even play the first chord! The fact that I couldn't do what every other guitar player was able to do remained a mystery to me. I would watch the beat groups on television, and they all were strumming their guitars easily, with fingers in the classic positions as displayed in my teaching book.

I was disheartened until I was told I had suffered from rickets as a child in Wales, and my wrist and arm bones had set differently from everyone else. It was then I realized I couldn't even turn my hands flat out in front of me as everyone else could. However, I discovered I could "cheat" and place my thumb over the top of the fretboard to play the low notes in the chord and use my fingers for the high notes. The six notes could then be played. Catastrophe averted! I practiced and did, in fact, take the guitar on a school outing. I could play chords and pick out individual notes within those chords. Friends would say I had some talent. I didn't believe them . . . couldn't anyone do what I was doing?

I then spent hours in my bedroom strumming to Elmore James records. I wouldn't even play in the same key. I'd just strum along with my fingers in a chord shape, and when I heard the music change, I'd change to another chord shape. I was, effectively, using the record as a metronome. I'd strum in time and make my hands change chords to the beat. It was a very good way to train my brain to communicate with my fingers. Pretty soon, I could change chords at will and in time to the beat. One of the other first things I did on guitar was to learn every note on the fretboard . . . there are quite a few. It was like learning one's multiplication tables as we had done in math class in the early school days. So, I now knew every note on the fretboard and could change chord shapes at will and stay in time as I tapped my foot to the Elmore James records. I also started to pick up guitar licks. The first solo I learned was from the record "Linda Lu" by Texas artist Ray Sharpe. I listened to a lot of Jimmy Reed and copied Lefty Bates, Phil Upchurch, and Lonnie Brooks, all the guitarists who played on Reed's *Live at Carnegie Hall* album. B.B. King and T-Bone Walker were the preeminent guitarists from previous decades, Walker in the 1940s and King in the 1950s. I studied them. In particular, Freddie King caught my attention because he wasn't sophisticated like B.B. and T-Bone. Freddie was out and out just pure energy and was a "hanging on one note" stylist. Blues playing is all about vibrato and how to make just one note sing, like a vocalist, simply by holding a single note and having it quiver with finger vibrato.

Learning to play guitar, to me, was like putting together a giant jigsaw puzzle. I often didn't know where it was all leading or what I was doing. I just went to the guitar every single day and attempted to learn something or, at least, practice what I already knew. I learned the opening chords to "Take Five" by the Dave Brubeck Quartet. That song had a blues tinge to it and was in 5/4 time. That was my introduction to the technical side of playing guitar by using different time signatures. "Green Onions" was another simple guitar riff I had under my belt. The "Bo Diddley beat" was one of the first things I could strum well. A local friend booked a band for a wedding and got me in as the guitarist. We played songs with that "Bo Diddley beat" all night . . . it was the only thing I could effectively play! I now believe that once you think something and practice that something (it can be anything), you can become that something! Want to be happy? Think it, do it, be it! That is a gross simplification, but given favorable circumstances in life, I'm not far wrong. The fact of the matter is, I really did not have an ear for music at all. In those early stages, I could hardly differentiate one note from another as I practiced on my first guitar.

The idea of me playing music started to grow inside me while practicing after going to see the stars on the package tours (particularly the Rolling Stones), listening to my brother's records, and watching musicians on television. By 1963, the Rolling Stones and the Yardbirds were London bands that I followed. I guess, after seeing Mick Jagger sing, I got the idea that I could sing. Little did I know. At that time, I read all the music papers, *Melody Maker* in particular. It was there that I saw an advertisement by a band looking for a vocalist and decided to apply for the gig. Of course, in those days, at fifteen years old, I don't think I even knew what the term "gig" meant.

Prior to going for the audition, I practiced singing Chuck Berry's song "Maybelline." There were a lot of lyrics to learn about cars and a girl. All the kids around me were listening to the first Bob Dylan records. Quiet, acoustic folk music wasn't my thing. I wanted electric loud music . . . and even Dylan wanted that himself a couple of years later! I sang my Chuck Berry song for my older brother, Harry. I had never sung before, not even in the bath. He must have thought I was mad, but didn't say anything.

At the time I was preparing for the audition, I was living with my parents in Wandsworth, South West London, in the row house on Marcilly Road. Getting a car ride was out of the question. The family didn't own a car, but public transport was always efficient and close at hand. Harry took me to the bus stop on the day of the vocalist audition. As we waited, Harry asked if he could hear my voice.

"Sing the song for me," he said in his lilting Welsh accent. He leaned toward me, and I began singing into his ear: "Maybelline, why can't you be true / You've started back doing the things you used to do." It sounded good to me. There was no response, and I took that as a positive! However, he did seem perplexed. Watching a concerned look on Harry's face, I boarded the bus and blithely went off, ignorant of my lack of talent. I was going to sing with a band! Harry wished me good luck one more time as the #49 red double-decker bus drove on down Wandsworth High Street. I sat in my favorite place, up top in the front seat. We passed the pub known as the Beehive as well as the Granada Theater and were soon heading to another part of the city.

I don't remember the area of London I went to, but it was typical for the time, with old, dirty brick industrial buildings suggesting a better past than the present we were living in at the time. Many of the streets wouldn't be gentrified for decades, and the pallor of the Second World War was still in the air. Bombed-out areas were still all around. The old buildings and homes I passed still had a timelessness about them. After getting off the bus, I walked for some time until I came to the address I had been given. Surprisingly, I was not nervous, and it's always that way until you have the experience and realize what can go wrong with a project. That's when the nerves start jangling. However, at age fifteen, with no worldly experience to draw on, I was as confident as a bull in breeding season.

I still recall singing at the audition. I can see myself onstage with the band. I had no idea what I was doing! The band started, and it sounded good and loud. The managers sat out front watching. I stood in front of the microphone and warbled away . . . timidly. I sang my Chuck Berry song with more hope and faith than technique. Nothing ventured, nothing gained was my mental state of mind. The song finished. Not much was said . . . I suppose nothing had to be said. I understood. I wasn't going to be the band's singer. I wasn't good enough. In fact, I wasn't a singer at all! This fact didn't upset me. There was no hand-wringing or tears. I was flying on a wing and a prayer, and I knew that deep inside.

The musicians were very sympathetic, and one of them, the youngest, escorted me back to the bus stop at the end of the road. He was kind, and we engaged in small talk.

"Thank you for coming. It went well. We'll call you," he lied. "Thanks. See you," I replied.

I replayed the events in my mind all the way back home on the bus. It was as if it was a dream. I asked myself if it really happened. Days and days went by, and, of course, I received no phone call. I got on with my life. Later, I saw the band on television. I don't think they became a household name, but they gave it a good try.

Back home, the next morning after the audition, Harry asked how it had gone. I mumbled a noncommittal few words in reply and went back to my bedroom. Actually, my bedroom was one we both shared. I comforted myself by turning on the small electric heater. The two horizontal bars glowed red. I lay down, trying my best to block my mind from the previous day's events. At least, I now knew I wasn't going to be a singer. It would have to be the guitar that would take me into a musical future. Looking back, I believe that whole experience, although I must have embarrassed myself, set me up for these fifty-plus years of a music career that I've had. I certainly realized that if you want to get ahead, you can't be afraid of embarrassing yourself! From that point on, for many, many years, I stuck to playing guitar.

This was also about the time I met my first girlfriend. She made me feel very worldly; perhaps due to my first sexual experience. When we first made love, in her bedroom at her parents' house, I had no idea what I was doing. I was so dumb. Eventually, I got the idea and looked forward to our regular trysts. The relationship ended when I decided I did not want to get myself deeply involved at such a young age of fifteen years old. She was a year older than me and deeply distraught when I left her. I told her goodbye, and, as in a movie, she ran after me in the rain. I didn't waver.

When you look back, you see that a number of things play into the decisions we make. In my case, the indifference I had for schooling, an awakening of my manhood, and the ongoing parental bickering had a hand in my next move. On top of all that, I also had dreams of traveling and playing guitar. Taken together, these things led me to leave school at fifteen. I was given a copy of the New Testament at the end of the leaving ceremony, and I still have it in my bureau. However, I have very little else from 1963. So, I was now what they call a dropout. At the time, I didn't care what anyone thought. I was ready to try my hand in the real world.

Shock! I soon found out I wasn't prepared for the real world. I knew I had to get a job. I looked around and was accepted at a local Italian barbershop to apprentice as a hairdresser. I didn't follow up on that. I pushed a barrow at the local market in Clapham Junction. Eventually, I landed a job packing boutique fluorescent lights for a small company in Streatham. Two elderly gentlemen, one in his eighties, also worked there. It was the three of us in a small factory packing the lights. I enjoyed it. I've always enjoyed the company of octogenarians. There's an amazing amount of genuine history to be learned from them. Still, though it was comfortable and a job, I knew I was going nowhere. It occurred to me that I'd be better off with a job that offered a pension and security. That led to me taking the civil service exam, passing, and being accepted into the Ministry of Defense (MOD). At first, I worked in the old War Office building, a large neobaroque building on Horse Guards Avenue on Whitehall in London. That closed in 1964, and I moved to the Main Building on Whitehall in Westminster, London. Here's a British dictionary explanation of what the MOD actually does: "The Ministry of Defense (MoD or MOD) is the British government department responsible for implementing the defense policy set by Her Majesty's Government and is the headquarters of the British Armed Forces."

For the first time, I felt that I was set for life. The second time came later on, in a bar in an American city after I signed a new record contract . . . but I'm getting ahead of myself. I was a junior clerk, or did they call it an assistant clerk? In my office, there also were two executives (a man and a woman) and a senior clerk. My job was to file papers and keep track of everything. Most of the men, including the higher executive Captain Harding in my office, were World War II veterans and, often, war heroes . . . men who thought they were never coming home but were now grateful to be behind desks. I had a top security clearance that allowed me to handle sensitive files, many of which I would hand-deliver to 10 Downing Street, home of the prime minister. There were no barricades in 1964, just a policeman standing by the front door. I'd knock, be let in, and hand over the files.

I was happy at my job, commuting to the center of London by train, wearing a suit and tie and walking through St. James Park to start the day. I dated a couple of girls who also worked in the offices. After work, I'd walk one of them along the side of the Thames, which ran behind the MOD building. It was a nice life. I even survived another life-threatening event. I was walking home one evening and, as I crossed the main road, I was hit square on by a motorbike. I went 10 feet into the air, and as I did so, I had the presence of mind to find my balance in midair to come down standing on my feet. I was fine. The motorbike rider was also okay. "Blimey, mate; are you all right?" he asked anxiously.

"I'm perfectly fine," I replied, believing my own words: "How's your bike?"

He showed it to me: "Not a scratch, mate."

There was a small dent, but he wasn't worried. I was happy to walk away in one piece, so we shook hands, and I hurried to the station to get home on time. Back home, I began to experience some of the aftereffects. I must have been suffering from shock. I was lightheaded. My mother made me a cup of tea. I stayed up, watched television, and went to bed. The next morning, I went to work as usual.

# CHAPTER 5

## EPIPHANY, FEELINGS, SOUL, THE BLUES, AND MY GUITAR SOUND

All that we send into the lives of others
comes back into our own.
—Edwin Markham

Pop music, while all around me in the 1950s, with songs on the radio by Tony Bennett and others, didn't really leave a mark on me. Although I did enjoy the Bennett songs and other lighthearted tunes I heard on BBC radio, it never sparked a fire in me. My actual first musical memories, apart from listening to brother Harry's 78 rpm records, were of Sunday mornings with my mother making a Sunday roast dinner while the Billy Cotton Band Hour would be playing on the radio.

Later on, as an early teenager, my musical taste was more varied. It consisted of a mix of rhythm and blues, rock and roll, jazz, and blues. I liked the Top 20 songs and I joined in with the crowd, but deep down, I liked music with a more emotional punch. I wanted something with soul, and by that I mean something with a tinge of American southern Black culture. I wanted gospel and blues roots in my music. I found that sound in the music of James Brown, the Isley Brothers, Buddy Holly, Elvis Presley, Jerry Lee Lewis, and, well, the list could fill a page.

Then one day in 1963, I heard "You Shook Me" by Muddy Waters. The song featured Earl Hooker playing slide guitar in regular tuning rather than traditional bottleneck tunings such as Sebastopol and Spanish. In fact, the tune was an instrumental that Hooker himself had recorded, before Chess Records simply added Muddy's vocal to the track. It was in the classic Chicago blues style of music. It was such a great song that it may have been the inspiration, lyrically, for a later AC/DC song, "You Shook Me All Night Long." Whether intentional or not, I liked the AC/DC song because it had that blues root. Earl Hooker's guitar on the original track was sheer poetry to my ears. The whole composition, the vocal and the guitar playing, brought on an epiphany to me. Yes, I loved all the music I had been listening to, but it was the Chicago blues style, with the singing guitar, played with a melancholy vibrato, that I really wanted to hear . . . and eventually specialize in as a musician.

Most of the Chicago musicians I started to focus on had migrated from the southern states because work could be found in abundance in the northern cities. In addition, Chicago was a blues hotspot. After hearing "You Shook Me," I studied blues music as if I had received a calling from God. Perhaps, I HAD been called. One of my favorite artists was Howlin' Wolf. It seemed his voice was majestic and rough and ready for anything. He also played simple, but great, harmonica. His style was citified, but only a half step away from the delta where he grew up. At the time, he was very much a fringe artist and nowhere to be found on the mainstream map. If you told me in the 1960s that he would, someday, have a postage stamp honoring him, I would have said you were mad. Unfortunately, Earl Hooker, one of the greatest slide guitar players in electric blues ever, lives on and is truly appreciated only in the minds of aficionados. I dreamt of being Earl. I never wanted fame. I wanted greatness, and often the two don't mix except for in a chosen few. Besides, the mantle of fame is often too heavy a load to bear.

Earl Hooker's style was sparse, tuneful, and without bombast. If I may go off on a tangent for one moment, today's guitarists, not all of them, of course, tend to favor too much technique. For instance, they'll play fast to wow an audience. At times, it seems that very few, if any, of the younger generation know of the word "economy" in a musical sense. Space is very important in soloing. Unless you are a total genius who can make sense of a hundred notes, it's better to stick to five.

To get the Earl Hooker sound, I studied vibrato, which was achieved by bending strings upward to make the notes sing like a vocalist. B.B. King was also someone I studied for technique, although B.B. often played too smoothly for my taste. I liked tough, mean, distorted blues! That's where guys such as Freddie King came into the picture, with the much more overtly emotional playing style.

That's been my best attribute on guitar. I am an overtly emotional player. However, it's not a pose or something I've learned. I'm not copying someone else or displaying a practiced style. It's just my personality coming out through the instrument.

It was in the early 1960s that blues guitar, as played by Caucasians, started to come into its own. There was Lonnie Mack, Eric Clapton, Mike Bloomfield, and Steve Cropper. They were guitarists who were ahead of the pack. I was younger and close behind. I had to develop my own style to compete and also to show what I had inside. I knew, within myself, that I was different from anybody else. I had my own unique soul (everyone does), and I wanted to show that through guitar notes. That's what Earl Hooker had done.

Later in the late 1960s, Jimi Hendrix had a plethora of guitar sounds. He would experiment with foot pedals such as wah-wah and fuzz tones. I decided I couldn't compete on that level. Instead, I went the way of the purist and simply used a guitar and amplifier without accessories. I'd manipulate the tones via the knobs on the guitar and amp. I could turn the amp up to volume 10 and get a distorted tone if the guitar was also at full volume. If I wanted a cleaner tone, I would simply turn the guitar volume lower or manipulate the amplifier settings. All my amplifier tone settings, bass, middle, and treble, I'd have on 10 . . . all the way to the right. I preferred the Marshall 50-watt amplifier heads because the sound would "break up" better; that is, distort in the right way. What you didn't want is false distortion. When the 1970s came around, I'd hear that false distortion on record after record. Musicians, to me, just seemed to be faking it.

So, I was a purist sticking to a clean guitar sound overdriven by only an amplifier. It had been done that way ten years before I came along by guitarists such as Pat Hare on the old Howlin' Wolf recordings. I made a point of drawing an audience to me by standing quite still, with the guitar neck straight up and next to my face. I did that to show that I was bonding with the instrument. In addition, I wore fringe jackets, snakeskin boots, and clothes that would draw the eye toward me. I was creating an aura, or so I hoped, without trying to be flamboyant. I was shy, so I didn't try to be something I wasn't. I think I am playing very well these days, but my young-man playing reached its zenith in 1969. Have I told you that was my favorite year?

The guitar tone has always been my benchmark, and it still gives me great pleasure when other musicians say they like my tone. It's not easy to get a guitar tone that sings and hits people's hearts. It is all tied in with your personality and your character. If your playing doesn't have personality, it doesn't matter how technically accomplished you may be . . . you'll never be a great blues player. To leave a mark, especially with the cognoscenti, you have to play with personality and an individualism no one else has.

I always emphasize the middle tones of the music spectrum in my guitar sound. Blues, again to me, should have a deep sound . . . it comes from deep inside and needs to be warm and encompassing. This is my taste, of course. I want my vocalists to sing in deep tones. I want the music to be "heavy." I'm not so keen on treble and high-pitched sounds in my blues. Of course, I love certain players who go against what I'm saying, but my personal preference is for the middle tone and bass musical spectrum.

I believe it was the emphasis on the warm guitar sound that exemplified the British blues sound of 1965–66, which led to the 1968 British blues boom. The boom collapsed after a year, I believe, partly because too many nonblues musicians jumped on the bandwagon and partly because it was just another fashion trend . . . the kind that is commonplace in Britain regarding any musical genre.

When I came along to the music scene, the blues tone, of which I was and still am a proponent, left many old-school players floundering in another era. Tinny, treble-sounding guitars were suddenly a thing of the past. Before you knew it, even American players were copying the British style. Mike Bloomfield changed from a Fender Telecaster to a Gibson Les Paul with its thicker sound. It is interesting how the guitar sound originated in America, was tweaked by us British guys, and then was brought back to its homeland to be reinvented to bring new life and energy to the genre. Some American musicians resent this fact and will tell you that only Americans can play the blues. I believe that anyone, of any color and nationality, can play the blues. However, there are only a few who touch the hearts of the public at large.

Listening to my record collection, living so far away from America, across the Atlantic Ocean, I could tell who the great, not-so-great, and average American blues musicians were. The distance gave me objectivity. Even so, I listened and studied all of them. Sometimes, you learn more from a not-so-great player than you do from the A-list types.

I particularly liked John Lee Hooker's style of playing because it was heartfelt and primitive. In fact, I've always liked primitive art and folk art of any kind. Hooker, in fact, a distant relative of Earl Hooker, wouldn't even rhyme lines within a verse, and whereas blues music generally falls within a twelve-bar musical structure, Hooker would often play eleven or thirteen bars. It jarred me as a listener who had been brought up to believe that "moon" rhymed with "June." Hooker broke those rules, either deliberately or instinctively. I'd play his records in my parents' sitting room, in the dark, absorbing the intensity of his voice and guitar. Plus, he was a great songwriter. That's another thing—no matter how good a guitar player you are, it doesn't mean much in terms of longevity unless the guitar is played within the context of a good song. A good song is what is remembered. It is the skeleton on which you hang a guitar track. "You Shook Me" is a fine example of that.

Lightnin' Hopkins was another electric country blues artist I adored for his "make it up as you go" style of blues. Lightnin' Slim, who seemed to trade on the Hopkins style, was another "down-home" player I liked. I couldn't imagine that these artists actually existed in the world, because it was a world far removed from anything I'd ever experienced. That unworldliness added a sort of romance to their existence and artistry. It was artistry easily missed if you weren't looking closely. A lot of young Americans my age weren't paying particular attention until British musicians, such as myself, made them prick up their ears and wonder where the music we were playing had come from. They were surprised it was from around their back door.

The blues I first listened to had honesty, had little affectation, was accidentally commercial (if it was at all), had conviction, and had soul. It was almost cosmic. It was accidental in its form. It spoke to me. It still speaks to me. Champion Jack Dupree once said to me, "If you play boogie-woogie, you'll always make a living." For some of us, truer words were never spoken.

# CHAPTER 6

## MODS, LONDON MUSIC SCENE, FIRST ELECTRIC GUITAR, AND ERIC CLAPTON

I think continually of those who were truly great.
—Stephen Spender

Living in Wandsworth, London, with my parents as a fifteen-year-old, I was surrounded by Mods, many of whom were part of the gang of guys I grew up with and had gone to school with. Mods were a generation of teenagers and twenty-year-olds who listened to R&B, rode scooters, and dressed smartly. At first, in my area, they had eighteen-gear, drop-handled racing bicycles, and, as they grew older, those were replaced by Italian motor scooters. I was envious. They were older boys, perhaps by two years. I could only watch it happen until it was my time. Pretty soon, I, too, was a Mod. I had my Clarks desert boots on, and I wore a striped mohair jacket. I also had a neat and buttoned-down check shirt. I enjoyed dressing as a Mod. I also wore hooped, long-sleeved sweaters that I hoped would make me look bigger.

On Friday nights, an entire street corner, at the end of my street, would be filled by a hundred Mods wondering where, and how, the weekend was going to start. Everyone was looking smartly dressed and they were "Street Corner Talking." I would look on from a distance. A year or two difference separates you quite a bit at that age.

Among all of this, I listened intensively to blues music and studied the genre. It was already in my bones from a decade of listening to my brother's record collection. The year culminated in my leaving school at the conclusion of the school year in September. I wanted to make my mark on the world. My thinking was that I couldn't waste any more time in school. The Beatles had released their first album and were on top of the charts. Every song they released went to number one . . . there were three that year. The Rolling Stones had released their first single, "Come On," a record I immediately bought.

I was deep into listening to American blues and enjoying the rhythm and blues that was now starting to envelop the British music scene. I wanted to be a part of this new music explosion. I instinctively felt that the blues guitar I was hearing on my brother's imported American records was going to be the new future of music. However, blues, rhythm and blues, rock and roll, and jazz were all part of a whole. I hadn't had that eureka moment yet when I would separate Chicago blues from all other music and know that was the music for me. However, that moment was coming.

From the age of thirteen, I practiced solidly for three years in between playing soccer and going to the local pool hall. Oh yes, the pool hall was a great place to glimpse another world set apart from the humdrum streets of South London. Harry was a supergood player, but I was not . . . yet another sport I failed at. But Eureka! By the time I was sixteen, I could play guitar! I thought I was some kind of genius, but it was just dedication and hard work and had nothing to do with "genius." Eventually, the picture was becoming clearer to my adolescent mind. I wasn't going to be a soccer player or a sportsman, and I wasn't going to be a singer. I was going to be a guitar player, and not just any guitar player . . . I was going to be a blues guitar player.

It was during this time that I became a Londoner. My Welsh accent was long gone apart from the occasional pronunciation of "year" instead of "here." My thinking started to evolve as I became a sophisticated city guy. I was modern. I liked cutting-edge poetry. I practiced yoga and learned the proper breathing techniques and exercises that have lasted a lifetime. April was my favorite month. My favorite poem was "The Waste Land" by T. S. Eliot. My favorite guitarist was Freddie King. However, underneath it all, because of my Welsh background, there was still a part of me that didn't quite fit, and I had a tendency to daydream. Often, I would find myself looking in from the outside, a theme I wrote about in a later song, the title track of the album *Looking In*.

To help my musical development along, American blues acts were now touring the UK. I saw Howlin' Wolf at the Marquee Club, with Hubert Sumlin on guitar. Hubert was playing an odd guitar, and that fact remained in my mind for years. I couldn't imagine what guitar he was playing. I finally got the answer in the 1990s, when I played on a solo album of his. I asked him about that gig in London all those years ago, and he told me the story. He had been in Germany and had given his expensive Fender Stratocaster to somebody on a whim as a gift. He then needed an instrument and went to a pawn shop and bought a fifty-dollar guitar! That was the kind of person Hubert was.

I saw Jimmy Reed at the Flamingo Club. It was one of my favorite clubs in Soho. I took a girlfriend to see a show, and, to be a gentleman, I had to dance with her and show her attention. However, all I really wanted to do was watch the great bluesman play. She really wasn't there for the music. All she wanted was a fun night out in Soho. At least I can say I danced to Jimmy Reed! I'd often go to the Flamingo. It was an all-night venue that catered to a lot of Jamaicans since it often featured bluebeat, a popular Jamaican-based R&B music. Among that, I would see the Zoot Money's Big Roll Band with Andy Summers on guitar, and Chris Farlowe's band with guitarist Albert Lee. During those late nights, looking baby-faced and as young as I did back then, I'm surprised I wasn't mugged or otherwise set upon. I guess it was a different world at that time. I did have to ignore older gay men who seemed to be attracted to me. I suppose the reason was that I was a small-sized pretty boy. I would often have to ignore them as they got uncomfortably close in public lavatories and would even sit next to me on late-night buses. I would simply pretend they weren't there. Presumably, with the gay lifestyle now accepted within mainstream society, that kind of thing is long gone. I guess it was all part of life in the big city . . . at least in those days.

I was practicing on the guitar, listening to music, and watching bands play around London. My local church hall was one of the venues I frequented to hear bands play. Many touring bands played there. I particularly liked the Downliners Sect. They had a great smoky sound and played cover songs such as the Coasters' "Little Egypt" and Chuck Berry's "Beautiful Delilah." Watching the Downliners Sect was the first time I could feel the music, particularly the bass, coming loud from the stage and throbbing through my whole body. The church hall stage was about 6 feet off the ground, and the audience would have to stand since there were no chairs. I usually went on my own, and I'd wear two or three sweater tops in an attempt to hide my painfully thin body. I figured I'd look more manly wearing a full wardrobe. Alex Harvey was another interesting act that played at the church hall. I had read about him in the music papers. He was from Scotland. I thought he was good, and he certainly looked experienced onstage. The next time I saw Alex play was in the early 1970s in Los Angeles. By then, he was very popular in the UK but never did quite conquer America. That particular night in California, he had obviously been drinking, and upon walking onto a table in front of the stage, dressed in pirate clothes, complete with sword, he promptly toppled over and hit the floor. He got up and soldiered on with a bent sword at his side. It was marvelous fun from an audience standpoint, and I think they thought it was part of the show.

Wimbledon Palais was another venue I would go to. It was an interesting ballroom with two stages. On one stage, an older-fashioned big band would play. On the main stage, the popular "beat groups" of the day would perform. The Beatles played there, and so did a lot of the northern English acts when they came down to London. I saw many of them, and I was particularly interested in the guitarists with good reputations. I went specifically to see Mick Green play with Johnny Kidd and the Pirates. Green was fantastic, playing lead and rhythm guitar simultaneously on a Gibson double-cutaway guitar. The opening act on a few of the bills was the English band the Outlaws. They had a fine guitarist, Richie Blackmore, and I knew he was destined for greatness. He played a red Gibson 335 and had a moody vibe onstage. Richie went on to form the great rock band Deep Purple. Ten years later, in 1974, my band would be special guests on a massive American tour with them.

I also went to the Scene Club in Ham Yard, Soho. It was a club that had opened in 1963 and was a place the first Mod bands, such as the Who, had played. A friend told me about the Who and informed me that they smashed their guitars onstage. It was ludicrous to think a band could be such anarchists! I went to the club hoping to see something of the new scene. However, the Who was not playing, and I got to see Georgie Fame. Fame had a cool jazz presence and vocal style. He hunched over a Hammond organ with eyes that looked like they hadn't seen sleep in days. No one was there that night. It must have been midweek, and the room was empty. I sat on the benches surrounding the perimeter, close to the walls. No one was on the dance floor.

However, the DJ played an amazing song between the live music sets. It was "Memphis" by Lonnie Mack. I couldn't believe the guitar playing. I bought the single the next day. No one in the world was playing like Lonnie . . . so fast, so soulfully, and with such dexterity.

The Marquee Club was another club I often frequented in Soho on Wardour Street. The Yardbirds played there with Eric Clapton on guitar. Clapton was marvelous, and I was a fan of the band. I also enjoyed singer Long John Baldry's band when he played there. Rod Stewart was doing some of the singing in Baldry's band at that time, and he would get heckled mercilessly because of his feminine haircut. It was well known that Long John was gay, and Rod got teased by association.

At some point, I decided to purchase an electric guitar. I spent some time window-shopping cheap guitars such as the Futurama and Rosetti models. I was accustomed to buying records at the Readings Music Store in Clapham Junction. They also happened to sell the cheaper-line European-import guitars. Initially, a lot of the new beat groups played these types of instruments, whereas, most of the time, the musicians I was watching played American-made guitars. As a result, I knew what I was looking at in the window of my local record store . . . and it wasn't quite the real thing. Eventually, I found a Hofner guitar that looked like it was close to a professional instrument. The model was a Hofner Verithin, and it looked very much like a Gibson ES-335. It was a beautiful red color. What more could any sixteen-year-old want? Not having enough money saved, I could buy it only on hire-purchase, but the music store wouldn't allow me to go ahead with the paperwork. I was too young. I was upset, and my dad stepped in and paid cash for the guitar. It was the first of many wonderful things he would do for me as I moved on through life. I fixed up a small amplifier to go along with my Hofner guitar, and I practiced and practiced. I would play every day even for just a few minutes. I was moving forward step by step toward an unknown future and a destiny beyond my wildest imagination.

My own record collection was starting to grow. The first single I bought was "Twist and Shout" by the Isley Brothers. I loved the B side, which was an instrumental version of the song with which most of us are familiar. I loved the drumming. With my record collection and my new electric guitar, I felt like I was making the first step to achieving a dream that was still somewhat cloudy in my mind. Rhythm and blues was the going-on music sound . . . even pop hits had an R&B flavor. The Beatles, the Rolling Stones, the Animals, the Who, the Kinks, and the Small Faces were the toast of London. They all had hit records on the charts. I'd watch them on television, not knowing I'd be joining them, after a fashion, very shortly. I liked them all, especially the Beatles. I was a fan of the Rolling Stones, but I never tried to play any of their hit songs. It wasn't the music I wanted to play. I wanted to play Chicago blues. The UK pop music, rhythm and blues, American South gospel music, Louisiana zydeco rhythms, funky James Brown, Elvis Presley's rock and roll, and modern jazz were the mixture of sounds I was listening to. However, as a musician, I wanted to play simple blues. I was single-minded in that regard. I had blinkers on. Nothing else mattered. I was on a mission. You won't see my name or the band's name much in written history detailing the UK blues explosion that was going to happen three or four years later, but, undoubtedly, I was one of the first people to drive it on with the Savoy Brown Blues Band, the group I was soon to form.

Muddy Waters was a big inspiration. He WAS the Chicago blues sound I wanted to emulate. The song "You Shook Me" was my turning point. All of my musical influences crystallized down to one central point . . . Chicago blues.

"Green Onions," by Booker T. & the M.G.'s, was a huge instrumental hit in 1963. It must have been, and perhaps still is, the first thing many aspiring rock and blues guitarists learn to play. Steve Cropper was a wonderful player. He had a strangled, minimalist style. Totally original. I copied him. Mike Bloomfield was playing in the Paul Butterfield Blues Band, and I was greatly influenced by him and the whole band. That group became my main focus. I wanted to have the British equivalent of the Butterfield band. I sounded a lot like Bloomfield. I had seen Eric Clapton with the Yardbirds at the Marquee Club. Then, one evening, I was walking on a London street, and I heard music coming from a house. The house was right next to the sidewalk, and I heard guitar music coming through the bay window. The music was great. I knocked on the door! A boy, my age, opened the door, and I asked him what he was listening to. He answered that it was the Yardbirds, and he had been playing the B side of the band's single hit record "For Your Love." "Got To Hurry" was the instrumental I had heard, and it featured Eric Clapton. It was the first time I had heard a British guitarist sounding as good on record as the American players I was listening to. Clapton was starting to leave an indelible impression. I bought the single for the B side. I never played the A side.

A short time later, Clapton had left the Yardbirds . . . it seemed the band was going in a commercial direction, and he wanted to play traditional blues. I read in a music newspaper that he was on a foreign jaunt of some sort, and Jeff Beck had replaced him in the band. The next time I saw the Yardbirds, at the Ram Jam Club in Brixton, Beck was playing guitar and Jimmy Page was playing bass.

Mostly, while I was getting myself and the band together, I would go to the Flamingo Club in Soho for inspiration. A lot of the bands with good musicianship played at the Flamingo. One night, I went to see John Mayall play. Mayall had a lighter electric tone to his music that I had heard on his singles "Crawling Up a Hill" and "Crocodile Walk." As I was walking down the dingy stairs leading to the club in the basement, I heard the band playing. I heard something that I thought couldn't be John Mayall. The sound was too hard and heavy. The guitar sounded like a mix of Otis Rush, Steve Cropper, and Freddie King! I was excited. I had to find out who was playing guitar. I had heard nothing like it before in the London clubs. I paid at the door and walked in. There was a good-sized audience, but my eyes immediately went to the stage. It was John Mayall, all right, and the difference in the sound was that he now had Eric Clapton on guitar, Jack Bruce on bass, and Hughie Flint on drums. It seemed to me they made up what would later be called a "supergroup." They had an amazing sound together. The main sound, heavy, mean, and threatening, was coming from a Gibson Les Paul guitar that Eric was playing. It had a much-thicker sound than his previous Fender Telecaster. Yes, the guitar, along with the amplifier, gave him a new sound previously unheard of in Britain. However, more than anything else, it was his musicianship that was amazing. He had emotion and technique, and he could swing. It seemed to me that he had everything. After the set, I caught Clapton on the way to the dressing room, and, starry-eyed, I told him how great he was sounding.

After seeing Mayall and Clapton together, my school friend Chris Standen and I went to see as many John Mayall gigs as we could around London. Chris was a good friend of mine, and he got caught up in my excitement for listening and going to see blues music . . . specifically, going to see John Mayall with his new band. In fact, I recall Chris calling Clapton "God" before anyone else. I almost think he started that trend that led to the "Clapton is God" graffiti around London. Chris died in his fifties, and it's such a shame. I would have liked to have talked to him and gotten his reminiscences for this book.

Going to those shows, I would see every current name guitarist in the audience, as well as the up-and-coming names such as Jimmy Page, Big Jim Sullivan, and Robert Fripp. Jimmy Page got onstage one night and jammed. He must have been nervous, since he played as fast as he possibly could. He could really play, and I had never heard anyone play with such speed. Nevertheless, feel and style, two things Clapton had in abundance, were really what I was focused on. That was the essence of the blues to me.

In my own playing, I had the feel and the style but still had several questions concerning the missing parts of my playing. The three most important questions seemed to be about how one swings as Clapton did: How does one achieve the dexterity and how does one get the sound? Why is it that some can play the blues with feeling, and others simply play the blues as a music form? It's down to the personality of each individual, of course, but I do think one's experiences as a child come into play. If your life, when young, has had its troubles, there may be some pain or confusion you can pull from to express the blues, much like an actor is able to emote from dredging up events from their past. Also, in my case, I have always been a loner. My mother, by not letting me be one of the crowd, perhaps started me on that path. I don't know. Is that a reason for having the feeling to play the blues? Blues music is all about feeling . . . poetic feeling. It's not just a matter of playing notes with dexterity. The notes have to tumble beneath your fingers like beautiful waves . . . poetry in motion.

# CHAPTER 7

## I FORM SAVOY BROWN'S BLUES BAND, START A CLUB, AND RECORD FOR THE FIRST TIME

I am a shade and haunt still the place
where memories linger.
—Verner von Heidenstam

It was a rainy Saturday morning in 1965. I had caught the bus and gone to Soho, in London's West End, to buy records at Transat Imports, a small basement shop on Lisle Street selling imported American albums. It was open only on Saturdays, and open just in the morning. The week before, I had bought an amazingly rare album, at least one not available in Britain. It was called *Freddy King Goes Surfin'* and was an album of instrumentals by one of the leading American blues guitarists of that time.

It was a blues album released by King Records, and I can only guess, with the album title, that they were looking for a commercial promotion angle, since surf music was popular and selling well. It didn't matter to me what it was called. What could be better for a budding blues guitarist like myself than fifty minutes of guitar licks to copy and learn? It was a master class I bought for one pound! My brother was envious.

This Saturday, though, with the rain falling, I was early, and the shop hadn't opened. I was sheltering in the doorway. I watched the typical Soho morning unfold in front of me. Italian restaurants were opening, and smart-dressed girls were walking under umbrellas. Delivery vehicles were scurrying through the narrow streets. There was always something exotic in the air.

You expected to see a celebrity walk by, and there were hundreds of mysterious doorways, like the one I was standing in, that seemed to lead to adventure rather than a simple apartment. Nothing was mundane in Soho . . . even the pigeons seemed to carry a regal and sophisticated air as they sat on window ledges and scanned the streets for food.

A fellow customer stepped into the doorway beside me to get out of the rain. There was just enough room for the two of us. As we waited for the store to open, we started talking. I thought I was the only person to ever show up before opening time. We introduced ourselves, and the stranger's name was John O'Leary. I told John I played guitar, and he replied that he played harmonica and had actually met Little Walter. "You met Little Walter?" I said, not believing my ears.

"Yes," returned John, "he gave me a tip. He said a lot of the English harmonica players were shaking their heads to get vibrato instead of shaking the instrument."

Little Walter had toured Europe with the American Folk Blues Festival package in the early 1960s and had impressed me. As we continued to talk, it turned out that John lived close to me in South West London. We arranged for me to go to his house, and he'd play me some of his blues records.

It was a weekend morning when I went for that first record-listening session. A Young's Brewery horse and cart, carrying barrels of real ale, came by in the other direction on Wandsworth High Street. It was a team of immaculate draft horses pulling the huge cart to make beer deliveries to local pubs. It was a wonderful public-relations move and a treat to see. Upon my arrival at John's flat (I believe he was living with his parents), I saw a Cliff Richards album. This was hardly the esoteric record I was expecting to see. It was Cliff's first album, and his coiffured head filled the whole album cover. He looked like a typical 1950s teen idol . . . a copy of Elvis with a little James Dean thrown in. I had liked his first single, "Move It," but afterward, for my taste, his musical output quickly dissipated into insipid pop music.

"That was my sister's. I can't stand Cliff Richards. Too girly" were John's words, and I quickly knew where he stood regarding pop music. He pulled out some of his own records. Being a harp player, he had some great early James Cotton recordings. One of his prized possessions was an Otis Rush recording, a Cobra Records 78 rpm release, "Groaning the Blues."

There weren't many people in London, even in the whole country and, perhaps, the whole of Europe, with those kinds of records. I had found a kindred spirit.

John, an Irishman, dressed fashionably. He had long legs, dark curly hair, and an attractive personality. His demeanor always seemed to project a certain sadness. Perhaps it was his Celtic background; maybe it was due to his young sister dying of leukemia. I never quite understood his personality. He carried a brokenness and a world-weariness that appealed to me immensely. To top it off, he played harmonica wonderfully. Don't shake your head for vibrato, shake the instrument was a lesson John had long learned. John knew how to play.

I was also doing my best to know how to play. I listened to and copied Matt "Guitar" Murphy's playing with Memphis Slim. I also listened to and copied Ennis Lowery playing on Champion Jack Dupree's album. I studied Billy Butler playing with the Bill Doggett band. I already had Freddie King and Otis Rush licks in my repertoire. I was ready to form a band.

My neighborhood was mostly working class. I suppose my family was middle class, although we lived modestly. The social-class structure in Britain was a big thing. From your voice, others could detect your place of birth, your schooling, and your status. You had to have the right kind of accent to get on in life, as well as the good fortune to live in the right area and have the right kind of credentials behind you. However, that was beginning to change. Society was starting to become more cosmopolitan. Music had a lot to do with that. The Beatles, a worldwide phenomenon, spoke with northern accents and were loved. There was greater pressure in southern England, and London, to conform to a refined speech.

However, by 1963, Cockney accents were becoming fashionable. Musicians, particularly singers in bands, would often use a Cockney accent for the effect, perhaps, of being antiestablishment.

When my family moved to England, I had a strong Welsh dialect. I had a terrible time at school with my pronunciation. By the time I was living in central London, my accent had faded, and I was now speaking like a Londoner, with only an occasional word marking me as coming from Wales. It was odd for me to hear my voice changing, not only in timbre as I matured but also by its very nature. I had now become an Englishman.

I started to put a band together. Second-generation Jamaicans lived in my area and were my age. I befriended one of them, and his name was Leo Mannings. Leo lived with his family in the large flats close to me. He played drums and became a close friend. We spent a lot of time together, and he was a great supporter of my guitar playing. Leo had a mischievous smile and was always even-keeled, and despite being small in stature, he made up for that fact by having a strong presence that made him appear much taller than he was. He was happy, and that helped me enormously since his optimism buoyed my spirits. I couldn't have moved ahead without Leo's friendship and support. So, together with John and Leo, singer Bryce Portious and bass player Ray Chappell were added to the lineup. At about this time, the race relations act that outlawed public racial discrimination came into being. I was already doing my bit . . . I had the first multiracial blues band ever in the UK and, maybe, one of the first multiracial bands, period.

The concept of the group was to mirror the Muddy Waters Blues Band and to get that classic modern Chicago blues sound I was hearing on new releases coming from Chess Records. The Rolling Stones were the closest in sound to Muddy Waters, but they had moved into mostly mainstream commercial rock music. I was a purist blues lover. I felt I had something to say and wanted to express that through blues music, even though it had already been once around the London scene, with the Stones, under the banner "rhythm and blues."

You needed a piano player to really get that Chicago blues sound. John knew of Bob Hall, who had previous success with a band known as the Groundhogs a couple of years earlier. We found where Bob lived, and went to his house to see if he would join the band. We knocked on the door of a house in a nice suburban area, and Bob answered. He was not a tall man, and his manner was largely studious. He could have been a professor, a wine taster, or a successful attorney. He was short-haired and neatly dressed, wearing a comfortable jumper. He looked at us a little distantly. I explained why John and I were there.

"Will you join us and form a blues band?" I asked enthusiastically. I certainly didn't anticipate his reply.

"Absolutely not," said Bob. "I've already done it. Blues is over, and you'd never make any money anyway. Forget it."

That wasn't quite what I wanted to hear. I had no sensible reply. Was I that out of touch? Was it true that blues music had already died? Was I trying to flog the proverbial dead horse? His manner shook me a little, but my confidence came back.

"I understand," I replied. "Think about it, though. We'd love you to join the band."

We left Bob and wandered back into the night. We did not ultimately believe what he had said, and we didn't take his advice. I found another piano player, Trevor Jeavons, who was less battle weary. For a few months, at the very beginning, rehearsals went on with Trevor, and the band was taking shape . . . quickly. Bob did change his mind and joined the band not long after that first meeting. I have no idea what changed his mind, but I'm glad he did.

John knew of the Nags Head Pub in Battersea. It had an upstairs room where a folk club had once flourished. Folk music had waned by 1965. That boom was over, and even Bob Dylan was moving on. John and I spoke of the idea of opening our own club, a blues club, in that room above the Nags Head. We went to see the proprietor, and the first thing we asked was "Can we rehearse the band in your room, and how much would you charge?" He was very accommodating and a great guy. He said we'd be more than welcome to use the room. I think he was simply happy that somebody cared about his facility.

The building that was home to the Nags Head was built to last. It was a very large, solid, three-story brick structure. There was a candle factory across the road. The aroma from that factory was fierce, but once you were inside the pub, with the windows closed and a pint of beer in your hand, all was well in the world. I started rehearsing the band and selected songs we would play on the basis of what I knew would fit everyone's abilities. That way, everyone would look good, the band would sound like we knew what we were doing, and we'd be a success. That's the way I've run a band ever since. Play to your strengths and minimize your weaknesses.

I had an experience fifty years later that brought back those days at the Nags Head very vividly. I picked up my old Memphis Slim album, which had been collecting dust in an old box for many years. A slip of paper fell out. I could easily have tossed it away, but I looked at the frail and discolored sheet. It had a typed list of songs on it. I recognized something without first understanding what I was looking at. It was a set list from one of the first rehearsals at the Nags Head. The songs I had the band playing were a mixture of what are now considered blues standards. However, at that time, they had been recently recorded by the likes of Junior Wells and Muddy Waters. There were also compositions by Buddy Guy, Otis Rush, and Freddie King on the list. That's the music the band was rehearsing above the Nags Head Pub in the fall of 1965.

Having a place to rehearse was one thing. Getting the equipment to the room was another thing. By then, I had relegated my Hofner Verithin guitar to the "B" team and had bought a Fender Telecaster paired with a Vox AC 30 amplifier. It was the classic professional setup for that time period and can still be, for some, today. People often ask me what the difference is in the music business today compared to the 1960s. I tell them not much has changed. The equipment is exactly the same, and the players even look like they have stepped out of a 1960s photo of what a band should look like.

It's possible I started rehearsing the band in my bedroom, but that's just a fog in my mind. What I do know was we used a cab to get our equipment to the Nags Head Pub. A long, steep, and narrow staircase led to the upstairs room, and that was a problem. We needed to get an acoustic upright piano up those stairs, into the room, and up onto the stage. Bob Hall, myself, and the others gave it all we had. We managed to get the piano halfway up the stairs but got stuck at the slight turn in the stairway. The pub proprietor came to our aid. He didn't care about damage to the walls. He was having too much fun! We all were. So, we just pushed the piano up with wall plaster falling everywhere! Finally the piano was in place onstage, but not without leaving scars on us and the wall.

The Nags Head upstairs room had a stage at the far end that was elevated about 1 foot off the floor. There was some sparse seating around the walls. It was perfect to set up and rehearse in "real time" as if we were already performing. I think that was a key to my quick growth, and it accelerated the band's steady improvement. Rehearse as if it's for real, and then do it all over and over again.

"Dust My Broom," "Snatch It Back and Hold It," and "Going Down Slow" were songs in the band's early repertoire. I preferred material that featured a riff of some sort to serve as a musical hook. The lyrics themselves might also include a hook . . . the title, the story, or, preferably, both. I didn't think that songs with just a groove were strong enough in my world, and I tend to believe that to this day. I was looking for hooks of any sort. I was the first to bring Howlin' Wolf's "Ain't Superstitious," with its multiple hooks, to the attention of the UK, and it was not the last. A lot of the great blues songs of that time period were written by Willie Dixon, and I was a huge fan of Dixon's. Most R&B groups of the day did at least one Dixon tune. You'll find at least one on several Savoy Brown albums.

The band eventually worked up a show's worth of songs. I would spend hours going over each song in my head as I worked to formalize a stage plan. The day finally came. John and I were ready to open our own blues club and invite an audience. We needed a name. John, being Irish, thought of "Kilroy's." I was all for that, so small hand posters were made up, and we went around London sticking them up on poles in advantageous places.

I always thought we opened on a Monday night, traditionally Blue Monday, but that was my imagination at full throttle. I am told it was a Wednesday night. Now, Wednesday was, and still is, the worst night of the week for any band to play. We had set ourselves a hurdle right from the start. Obviously, the pub owner had his weekends covered but thought any help he could get attracting people to the pub midweek was a good idea. Therefore, the word went out and a few people actually showed up on the opening night. We put on the full show, and I loved it. You couldn't take the smile off my face as I played. What fun! Playing music you loved in front of an audience. It's something I've never gotten tired of. As the weeks and months moved forward, more and more people showed up until, one day, the band was playing to a full house. It caught on. The pub was packed. We were getting an audience, and the path to the future was set. We realized we needed someone to manage what was now a growing entity. Business wasn't a word in my vocabulary at that point in time. I thought that asking my brother to be the manager would be a good thing. He understood the music and had been a great inspiration to me growing up, personally and musically.

At the time I was considering my brother as the band's manager, Harry and Olwen were married and living in a house they bought on Harbut Road in Battersea. The area had a working-class vibe, and the road, a long side road, consisted of small row houses on either side. He lived upstairs on a self-contained two-bedroom floor and rented the ground floor to an older couple who had already been living at the house.

I asked Harry to come and see the band. He wasn't expecting much from his little brother, but he came along anyway. He later told me he was very surprised that I had such a good thing going. He jumped at the prospect of being the band's manager. At the time, he was working as a postman, but that didn't seem to be a problem. We were just having fun.

The first thing Harry did was to get the local paper to write a story about the new band playing at the Nags Head Pub. The pub became crowded quickly, and my mother was even recognized by a fan. "Haven't I seen you at Kilroy's?" she was asked.

"Yes, I'm Kim's mum," she beamed back.

The next thing Harry did was buy an old, used postal van that we used to get to our first travel dates. He drove to the first gig, and I think that's the last time I ever saw him drive. Harry didn't even drive the white E-Type Jaguar he had bought for himself later on when he had become a successful agent . . . he let others drive it. I guess he just had the Jag for show.

My brother was becoming quite the impresario and go-getter. He invited producer Mike Vernon to come to see the band at a Kilroy's performance. That led to the band recording some singles for Mike's Purdah Records label. Eric Clapton and Jimmy Page had recorded for the label, although I didn't know that at the time. Going to a professional studio for the first time became a good experience for me. At the recording session, I was so nervous I couldn't even tune my guitar. I hit the "E" note I needed on the grand piano. Then I played the open top string on my Telecaster. I tried to bring the sounds together, but I was lost. My nerves had put up a wall between my brain and fingers. Producer Neil Slaven came to my rescue and tuned the guitar for me. Once in tune, I settled down and went on to play some high-standard solos. People in the studio immediately likened me to Clapton.

"Wow, you're going to give Eric a run for his money, mate," Neil said. Even though I knew he was being kind, it was a good feeling knowing I had that kind of ability in me.

Eventually, Harry got a job as an agent at the London City Agency. He had badgered every talent agency for a job, without luck, until London City finally gave in. The agency gave him a phone and a chair in the hallway . . . he went on to become one of the country's best and biggest agents. He had the great gift of enthusiasm coupled with brash coarseness. He could always be expected to do the unexpected. Everyone was always surprised and taken off guard by his larger-than-life personality. "Money in yer hand" became his mantra as he explained that promises of payment were simply that . . . promises. He booked the band and all the agency's acts nonstop.

No wonder he was driving an expensive sports car in no time. It would be years before I bought my own car . . . a mini. Harry was also my personal manager, as well as the band's manager, but there was never a contract drawn up. It never occurred to us . . . at least it never did to me. I couldn't stand show business, and that was what Harry loved. It led to some terrible clashes between brothers who worked together.

# CHAPTER 8

## I QUIT MY DAY JOB AND START TO TRAVEL, AND JOHN CALLS IT QUITS

Things change. And friends leave.
Life doesn't stop for anybody.
—Stephen Chbosky

The Beatles were consistently having hits, and so were the Rolling Stones. Earlier in 1965, the Who released their first single, "I Can't Explain," and my favorite song, the Small Faces' first single, "Whatcha Gonna Do About It," was making waves. I was desperate to be a part of the great music going on all around me, but that didn't mean I would be jumping on any bandwagon. I was going against the grain and playing heavy, serious blues.

Before I knew it, 1966 came around, and for months I'd still play each week on York Road in Battersea at the Nags Head Pub. The band also had travel dates. We opened for Cream at their first London gig, and we played Eel Pie Island, the Flamingo Club, Klooks Kleek in North West London, and the famous holy-grail venue the Marquee.

The show with Cream was quite a feather in our cap. My road manager, Brian Wilcock, set the whole thing up. Brian was a Yorkshire man, growing up around the town of Leeds. He spoke with a slight northern accent, was unassuming, and loved music. He was a private man, and he got on like a house on fire with Harry. It was only natural that he should be part of the family. The gig was to take place at Klooks Kleek on August 2, 1966. Klooks Kleek was started as a jazz club by Dick Jordan in 1961. I played at the club many times, and it was located upstairs on the first floor of the Railway Hotel in West Hampstead, North West London. It had taken its name from a 1950s jazz album that was, interestingly, released by Savoy Records.

I was very nervous on that night opening for Cream. When we arrived, it was obvious we couldn't set our equipment up onstage. It was too small for two bands. Cream already had their equipment set up, and that included the double-bass drum kit belonging to Ginger Baker. He had started the band just a month earlier with Jack Bruce on bass and Eric Clapton on guitar. It was a three-piece supergroup, the first-ever supergroup. All three musicians were the cream of the jazz and blues musicians playing in England at the time, and that's how they got their name. It was decided we'd ask if we could use their equipment. I walked up to Eric Clapton in a full nervous mess and asked if I could play through his amplifier because the stage was too small to set my own up. I needn't have been so nervous.

"Sure, go ahead. It's all yours," Eric said.

I was amazed at how accommodating he and the whole band were. They let us use all of their equipment. We opened the show with the Elmore James song "Dust My Blues," and it went smoothly from there. The band and I acquitted ourselves well. I was told that Clapton was impressed, but I was far too shy to have a further conversation with him. I watched Cream's show, and it was loud and powerful. After all, there was a bank of Marshall amps onstage for a room that held a couple of hundred people. At the end of the night, I felt happy to have been a part of history. We would often also be the opening act to John Mayall's Bluesbreakers. We were on the bill with him numerous times throughout 1966 and 1967. It was a natural pairing considering we both had albums out on Decca Records. John was a difficult man to know. Harry and I once took records to his home for a get-together session, but it did not lead to friendships. I've been a fan all my adult life and have played lots of gigs with him during those years. Somewhere, he ended up opening shows for my band when we became famous in the United States. I still don't know him well. The times I have reached out to him did not prove to be fruitful. He remains an enigma to me.

I was very young when I started, and I was also a very precocious guitar player. I was very shy, but full of the knowledge that I had something to say with my guitar. I would be loath to strike up conversations with the other musicians, because I was unsure of my place in the world, and I was still coming to grips with the fact that I was in the same arena as the other bands I had only been reading about just months before. I have hardly said a word to my contemporaries from those days.

As my career was stepping up and the travel dates mounted, I was still working at the MOD government offices during the day. Unfortunately, my work was falling off, and I would be falling asleep at my desk because of the late nights playing gigs. I knew I had to make a decision. Should I quit the job? It was one of the hardest decisions in my life, and no one could make it for me. I tried to get advice at work from the older executive officers and ex-army men. They told me they never thought they would make it out of World War II alive. I guess they were trying to tell me that life is a gamble.

After much hand-wringing, I eventually did put in my resignation . . . I had no other option; my work rate was horrible. All of a sudden, I was a professional musician. My brother was handling all the band's financial business, and I was paid a weekly wage. I couldn't believe the position of freedom in which I now found myself, not having to work Monday to Friday from nine to five. After saying to my brother that every day now felt like a Sunday, I realized that I was now working seven nights a week. The difference was that it was a job I loved.

One gig during the 1966 period was opening a London show that had the Troggs as headliners. The Troggs were riding on a number of big chart hits that year, and I thought it was going to be an interesting show. I had now been in the music business long enough to be privy to the inside music gossip that circulated behind the scenes. Some of the gossip, watered down, made it to the newspapers. One juicy item was the bickering that went on between the members of the Troggs. I was never sure I could believe half the stuff that was coming at me through the gossip grapevine, but, sure enough, backstage at the show, all the Troggs band members were involved in a huge fight.

"Welcome to the big time," I thought.

The year went by quickly, and I found myself playing regularly. It was more of the same in 1967, with gig after gig. Jimi Hendrix had just released his first single, "Hey Joe," and that added weight to the exploding new guitar sound that was developing. I felt I was ahead of the curve, but my music wasn't as commercial as those around me. It wasn't rock and roll. It was the blues. Real blues. I didn't know it yet, but I was a purist and would never stop being such, although I did veer on and off the path as time went on. My thoughts were always to keep it simple. My life's mantra was the same. It was the key to life as I saw it. Don't overcomplicate. Reduce life to whatever it takes to make things easy to do. Know who you are, and adjust life to fit your personality. If you don't know who you are, you'll continue to do things that are counterproductive to your own self. That's no way to live or get ahead . . . happily, at least.

The hardest gigs to play, while I still worked the day job, were in Plymouth or Newcastle. Before the highways were expanded, those gigs meant a seven-hour drive back to London. At first, we'd drive overnight. Eventually, the budget would allow us to stay overnight, assuming we didn't have to be at work the next day. Hotels of any consequence were still not in the budget, so we'd stay in bed-and-breakfasts or overnight boardinghouses. George's, in Newcastle, was an old-fashioned overnight bed-and-breakfast/boardinghouse. It was a row house with no sign, and it took us ages to find it the first night. We were given the attic to stay in, and there were a number of beds. George would make breakfast in the morning. He was tall and, certainly, not garrulous. In fact, he hardly spoke a word. His cheek pallor was ghostly, and he always wore a greasy buttoned sweater.

The clientele was a mixture of show-biz types, actors, and prostitutes. I was young, and I thought it to be amusing.

In no time, it seemed, I was playing the London club scene. Throughout it all, I was helped along the way by my biggest fans . . . my parents, especially my mother. I would play quite a few of the London late-night "in clubs." The cream of London would drink and dance at these clubs until the early hours. Celebrities were in abundance, and the Chelsea-girl types would walk around with nothing on but a string dress, and the miniskirts were smaller than mini. The clothes designer Mary Quant had popularized the miniskirt dress in 1966, and it was creating a storm throughout the country. According to the church, it was the end of civilization as we know it.

It was quite the scene around London. Everyone was dressed in style. One night, I was playing at Blaises, a club in the basement of the Imperial Hotel in West London. Half-clad girls were walking around as the free spirit of 1960s London was in the air. I was playing onstage and feeling a part of the scene, even though I stood no chance of landing one of those dolly birds as a girlfriend. It was about 1:00 a.m., and I looked down. There, sitting at the front table, was my mother! I was all of eighteen years old and quite embarrassed. My dad and my parents' neighbors were also there. They were having a great time, but I wasn't. At that age, I couldn't figure out how my parents could possibly fit into swinging London . . . but they were determined, and they did!

The Speakeasy, on Margaret Street in central London, was a late-night watering hole for musicians, actors, and the swinging inner-city crowd. The evening didn't start until 10:00 and continued until 4:00 a.m. I played there quite a few times. The Steve Miller Band came in one night and jammed. I spoke to Steve, and he likened my playing to his own. They were impressive musicians. Boz Scaggs played rhythm guitar that night behind Steve and blew me away. I had never heard rhythm guitar played so well. They were in London to record the *Children of the Future* album at Olympic Studios. First, Steve Miller got up onstage, then Boz Scaggs, until finally the whole band took over the band stage. I, and my fellow bandmates, just sat in awe of this great American band playing songs for us and a few late-night stragglers. The drink of choice at the Speakeasy was the fashionable Scotch and Coke. I couldn't afford the prices, and there were no free drinks. That was just as well. I had my hands full performing without the distraction of alcohol.

On another occasion, the drummer of the Searchers, a northern hit pop group, got onstage to jam and was pulling faces and generally poking fun at the band as he hammed it up from behind the drum kit. Jeff Beck was in the audience. He got onstage and threw the drummer off. The night was saved. John Mayall joined the band for a jam on another occasion, but we were too loud for his liking. He kept trying to get us to lower the volume. He was fighting a losing battle. I wasn't about to be put in a box of someone else's making.

The Eel Pie Island Hotel, the Marquee Club, Klooks Kleek, and the Flamingo Club were other staples of my early gig itinerary with the band.

The Eel Pie Island Hotel was on an island of sorts in the middle of the River Thames. One of the only ways to get to the venue was over a footbridge. The hosts had a minicar that could fit on the bridge to cart our equipment, loaded on top, across the river. I played there on a co-bill with the great and legendary bluesman Champion Jack Dupree from Louisiana. Jack was also a London City Agency act, and we played many shows together while we were both at the agency. When we did dates together, the night started with a set from my band, and then Jack would take the stage with us backing him up. He played acoustic piano. In those days, circa 1966–67, there was always a piano at all venues. It was considered a necessity. It didn't mean those pianos would be in tune.

Many times, after our set, pianist Bob Hall would complain about the piano being out of tune and, sometimes, even have various keys missing. I would wonder how the headline act, Champion Jack, would be able to handle such bad equipment. I needn't have worried. It didn't matter what condition the piano was in. Jack knew how to entertain. He was the star, not the instrument. He always put on a great show, and he knew how to sing. One night, I was standing with him in the audience, at Eel Pie Island, watching another act on the bill.

"That singer won't last," Dupree said to me.

"Why is that? What do you mean?" I quizzed.

Jack replied, "He doesn't sing from the stomach. He sings from his throat."

He went on to explain to me the correct way of breathing and singing. I thought it funny when Jack's English wife would complain to me about the "wacky stuff" (marijuana) that Jack would smoke. Apparently, it was a regular routine.

"Really?" I replied, inwardly thinking how strange it all was.

Jack, living in a regular English town with a regular English woman, was living a remarkably unregulated life and, at the time, an illegal life. I laughed inside when she told me about her problems with Champion Jack, but, on the outside, commiserated with her and the problem. She noted that she didn't understand why he did it, because all it did was make him sleep.

The Marquee Club in Soho was an important showcase venue for any act that wanted to make it in the music business. One of the first, if not THE first time I played there, was in November 1966. I was opening the show for John Mayall with Paul Butterfield as a guest. John Gee was the manager, and he didn't hide the fact that he was gay. The first time I was on the Marquee stage was at the band's sound check in the afternoon of the show. I made sure my amp was working, and just before we were to try out a song, I quickly tuned up my guitar.

"Give me a G," I called out to harp player John.

Suddenly a hand clasped my shoulder.

"Here I am, darling. I'm all yours!"

It was John Gee making a funny pass at me. It was very funny, and I laughed with everyone else. It was commonplace . . . it seemed all gay people were attracted to me.

The Flamingo Club was also on Wardour Street in London's west-end section of Soho. It had a sleazy vibe, was notorious for its gangster connections, and became a Mod hangout. Like Klooks Kleek, it was originally a jazz club and was usually open all night. That usually meant playing until at least 4:00 a.m. It closed at 6:00 a.m. A small unassuming street door, with a sign above pointing to the club downstairs, was the invite. I had started watching bands play there in 1963 and in a short time became a performer on its stage. Things were moving faster and faster for me. As well as playing on home turf in Soho, London, I was now taking the band to towns farther afield on the outskirts of London. Quickly it became apparent that the band would be on the road playing and traveling.

John had the idea that he could bring his girlfriend, Valerie, in the van on the road. After one gig, we were both sitting on the floor of the van (there were no seats), and he proposed the idea to me.

"I'd like to bring Valerie with us," he said.

"I don't think that will fly," I stammered.

Although I was inexperienced, I knew that wasn't a working proposition. After all, we were going to work. These weren't going to be holiday trips. Realizing the situation he was in, with a good job on the line and marriage around the corner, John bowed out of the band. I have since heard that John had a fight with Harry at the time, over money, which led to his handing in his resignation. Either way, the writing was on the wall. It marked the end of our relationship, and we went our separate ways. We did not see each other again until thirty years later, when I returned to London to play the 100 Club. John jammed onstage with me that night, but the time together was a subdued event. A different time and place.

Now, with John gone, what to do? The band had recorded its first singles, gigs were coming in, and one of the key musicians had now left the band.

# CHAPTER 9

## FIRST PRO GUITAR, *SHAKE DOWN*, SACKED, AND THE SAVOY HOTEL

A flash of steely lightning from his hand,
Strikes down the groaning leader of the band.
—Walt Whitman

I used a Fender Telecaster as my first professional guitar because most of the guitarists I admired played one. They included Muddy Waters, Steve Cropper, Mike Bloomfield, and Eric Clapton. In addition, it was affordable since it was a lower-market-end guitar. American musical instruments were heavily taxed, and that made it hard on the pocket to buy in Europe. My guitar was cream colored, with a small, solid body and a rosewood neck. It was easy to play with the slim neck that fit my small hands, and its simple design appealed to my aesthetics. It had two pickups, with one pickup selector switch, one tone control, and one volume control. I've always been satisfied with that configuration. Why complicate things? Your talent should dominate the guitar. The instrument isn't the thing . . . you are. I played mostly on the front pickup to get a warmer blues sound. The general guitar tone in Britain at the time was much more to the treble side, and I preferred the warmer, jazzier tone of Matt "Guitar" Murphy and B.B. King. That tone emphasized the middle tones of the music spectrum. To rock out on fast tunes, or to attack more, I'd switch to the back treble pickup.

Eric Clapton was the first guitarist I heard playing live who exemplified that warm blues tone I was looking for myself. He accomplished that tone by also using a small, solid-body Gibson guitar. There was still a British snob value attached to using a larger guitar with f-holes like the American jazz players used. It looked like a "real" guitar that serious musicians should be playing. I was aware of this but belonged to a different generation. I was self-taught and serious but taking the world of guitar sound in a different direction. I played my Telecaster guitar all throughout the Nags Head Battersea days, on all the first gigs, on the band singles, and on *Shake Down*, my first album. It wasn't until 1967 that I decided it was time to change and move on to a different instrument.

My career was now moving forward. John O'Leary had now left the band. At first, I tried to find a harmonica replacement. However, there was no one as good as John to be found anywhere in London, and I didn't want to dilute the talent in the band by bringing in a poor substitute. I went in a totally different direction. I realize now that that is the best thing to do when facing band member changes. Don't disappoint yourself, or audiences, by trying to replicate what you've already done. So, I replaced John with a guitar player, Martin Stone. I had heard Martin on record with his own band, Stone's Masonry, and I had seen him around Soho looking smart and cool. He was skinny, had long sideburns, and always wore a Mod white plastic raincoat. He carried an air of being someone special. At the time, he may have been a junior newspaper reporter. Martin carried a small notebook with him at all times. He was different. He came from a suburban background and had a local girlfriend but cultivated a bohemian air that suggested he had lived an alternate lifestyle since birth. I had no idea what I was letting myself into when I had him join the band. I didn't have the experience to understand what chemistry among people meant, or that positive and negative forces are always at play in life. It would be my first understanding of what being in a band really meant, and an introduction to the vagaries and absurdity of human behavior.

With the lineup once again solidified, I took the band into the studio to record the first album, *Shake Down*. Harry had made a deal with Decca Records, and Mike Vernon was to be the producer. Mike had just recorded the John Mayall band, featuring Eric Clapton, that I was such a fan of . . . he had his finger on the pulse of the London blues scene. Vernon had seen me and the band play at Kilroy's, after being invited by Harry, and he seemed to be totally on our side. I'm sure that was one of the reasons Decca signed the band.

The recording session for *Shake Down* was at the main Decca studios in Hampstead. Again, I was very nervous going into the studio, and at the last moment, I changed my strings to a set of a heavier gauge. That turned out to be a big mistake, and I struggled through the whole week playing a guitar with strings that were too heavy and too tight. I just got on with the job . . . too much was happening so quickly around me, and I didn't want to hold things up by going to buy different strings. I had already turned up late for the first day, and Vernon had to reprimand me. I was never late again. In fact, the need for punctuality in the music business is the reason I am now "on time" to a fault.

Mike Vernon did a great job producing the band's first album. Gus Dudgeon was the engineer, and Roy Thomas Baker was the tape operator. Dudgeon went on to fame with Elton John recordings and, likewise, Baker with the band Queen. So, there was a lot of behind-the-scenes talent to bolster a young band in the studio for the first time. It was only recently that I made my peace with that first album. I played it and thought that it wasn't so bad. I realized that the heavier strings contributed to my guitar sound in a positive way, after thinking it was a negative all my life.

*Shake Down* is an album of mostly cover songs that have now become classic blues songs. It leads off with Willie Dixon's "Ain't Superstitious," which gave me the chance to show my guitar style. On the original Howlin' Wolf recording, guitarist Hubert Sumlin had played the main riff in a quirky manner. I straightened out the lick, and since then, everyone seems to be playing my arrangement. The song was the blueprint for the style of blues music I would make for the rest of my life. There's a heavy guitar riff, and the verses have a slight occult bent to them. There were occasional psychedelic overtones, but, above all, the record had a high-energy purist approach fueled by my own personality influence. High energy was the overall tone of the recording. Live, the band was overly loud, and that trait was also brought to the studio. Our amplifiers were dialed up to maximum volume. I covered a Freddie King tune, "High Rise," as one of the instrumentals, while Martin Stone wrote his own offering, "The Dormouse Rides the Rails." The album ends with an extended jam over the Fred McDowell song "Shake 'Em On Down." This was an arrangement brought in by pianist Bob Hall and was a stroke of genius on his part. The song allowed the band to go in a more rock direction, although that switch in musical style was frowned upon by producer Vernon.

It was a fascinating time to be in a recording studio. We had the capability to do only eight-track recordings. The songs were recorded live, and then the vocals were largely overdubbed. That side of the music business was in transition, with new ideas and studio equipment coming almost daily. Getting a good bass guitar track, however, was still a challenge. The low frequencies could provide a definite headache for engineers, and the musicians themselves weren't as highly trained as the previous generation. We were making it up, and the control room staff had to think on their feet.

I used public transport to show up each morning at ten o'clock for the day's session. The album was finished in a few days. The tea lady would arrive midmorning and midafternoon, pushing a trolley laden with biscuits (cookies), fresh tea, small sandwiches, milk, and sugar. We'd stop for tea twice daily and have lunch and dinner. It was amazing we could record an album with that kind of leisurely schedule.

*Shake Down* was the second Decca release featuring the new blues sound coming out of London. It followed John Mayall's *Blues Breakers with Eric Clapton*. Mayall's album came out a year before mine, and during that period, I'd often open shows for him. By that time, Eric Clapton had already left the band and had been replaced by Peter Green, followed by Mick Taylor. Clapton had left in 1966 to go a different path with Cream.

After recording an album, I never go back and listen to it. Not even once. I move on. I assume the album sold well enough, although I was not kept in the loop on sales, and I wasn't terribly interested in the business side of the band anyway. I left all that to brother Harry. The album release consolidated the group's reputation and made Harry's job of booking gigs easier.

One of the first major tours I did around this time was as a backup band for John Lee Hooker's 1967 British tour. At first, before the tour started, the Ram Jam Club in Brixton was rented for rehearsals. I was heavily into rehearsing the band, though I thought nothing of improvising on any certain night. Hooker flew in from America, and I had the band onstage waiting anxiously for him to arrive. We were quite familiar with the Hooker repertoire, so we weren't expecting any problems. It was the afternoon, and eventually Harry came in starry-eyed with John. After all, John Lee Hooker was one of the blues greats. Harry was beaming, but that turned quickly to a frown.

"What's this?" were Hooker's first words.

"We're ready to rehearse," I said timidly.

"I don't rehearse" was John's reply, and with that, he turned around and left the building, with Harry in confused pursuit. I learned that day that the older blues guys didn't rehearse.

So, we simply met John at the first venue and started playing. He made things up as we played. At one point, John and I were plugged into the same amplifier . . . one of us in each channel. When he played, I stopped, and when I played, he stopped. That way, we didn't overload the amplifier or get in each other's way. I once turned up with my hair dyed blonde and permed, with curls hanging all over my face and eyes. It was a passing fashion, and I had jumped on the bandwagon. John was standing outside the venue when I arrived, with one of his girlfriends (he always had girlfriends), and at first he didn't recognize me. Then, when he did, the look on his face was hilarious. I have no idea what he must have thought. He was certainly not ready for my transformation.

Hooker had an animalistic approach to music. His guitar playing was nontechnical and primitive. I wondered if his appeal might not stretch beyond the blues crowd, but we played all sorts of venues from clubs, armed-forces bases, debutante balls, and upper-class university bashes. Every audience loved him. What he had, his talent, his musical appeal, crossed all lines of society. He was astonishing in his ability to entertain any audience.

In the 1990s the guitar player in John's band told me that John had personally picked him up at the airport in San Francisco. He noted there was a Savoy Brown CD in the car. That pleased me. Once, in that time period, I went to visit Hooker at his Redwood home. Pete McMahon instigated the visit. Pete's band, the Kingsnakes, had backed up Hooker on several occasions. John played his new album for us and was very pleased with how it sounded. His dog was named Boogie, and that was appropriate considering the dog's master was the king of boogie music. John sat in his chair, and I noticed he was wearing his stage socks . . . black with white stars on them. The socks were part of his image and can be seen in many photos. I knew that Hooker took only one pair of socks on tour with him. He'd simply wash them daily and keep the packing to a minimum. Looking at him that day, I thought maybe that's all he had to his name . . . one pair of socks!

*Shake Down* did well on release, although it was not released at the start in the United States. The band continued touring, but personnel problems began to arise within a few months. Singer Bryce was failing. It seemed he was often singing out of tune and began showing an aggressive temperament. It was decided to replace him with singer Chris Youlden. Chris had previously worked with our bass player, Ray Chappell. More importantly, to me, was that Martin Stone was heavily influencing the band, much to my chagrin, both musically and personally. He had an insidious personality and, in my case, treacherous. He was pushing the band into a psychedelic music direction and had introduced drugs to everyone . . . speed and LSD. I tried both, once, and found they weren't for me. I didn't like introducing foreign substances into my body.

I thought the band was losing its original focus of Chicago blues, and this led to a bad situation. Everyone had sided musically with Martin and his progressive ideas. Then a crazy thing happened . . . brother Harry sacked me from my own band! Chris Youlden was now the singer in the band, with Martin Stone as the only guitarist and the de facto leader. The band did some gigs without me. I happened to be walking down the street one day as the band vehicle passed by on the way to one of those shows. I recall them publicly jeering at me as they passed by. It was humiliating and humbling.

The shows the band played without me brought problems that eventually involved the police. There were drugs involved in addition to general unprofessionalism. I went to Harry, sensing an opportunity. I explained what was happening inside the band regarding the drug taking, and what was happening to the band's musical direction. I could see Harry's mind turning inside a furrowed brow. Was he thinking of his brother? Was he thinking of his future? Was he thinking of money? I'll never know the answer to that question. However, I was persuasive, and he realized he had made a mistake by firing me, and the band was now on shaky ground musically and professionally. In those discussions, we decided I would return to the band with a different lineup. Chris Youlden would be kept on as the singer, but everyone else would be terminated. The band was, once again, still going to be the blues band I had always envisioned.

Chris singing and me playing guitar became the main focus of the new band. I added John Mayall's former drummer Hughie Flint and Bob Brunning on bass. The band continued to play regularly. Playing regularly meant anything from the Witches Cauldron (a seedy club in North London) to the smart "in clubs" of the West End, such as the Speakeasy and Blaises. In between, there were colleges, concerts, debutante balls, and, ah, yes . . . the Savoy Hotel. It seemed incongruous, right from the start, that a loud blues band, such as we were, should be playing at this esteemed and posh hotel. However, no one was going to turn down a gig. So, with assurances from Harry, our agent, that there was nothing to worry about, we packed our Vox amplifiers and Fender guitars into the trusty Ford Transit van and set out for the city.

Now, the Savoy Hotel was, and still is, synonymous with class and style. In fact, it had been the inspiration behind part of the band's name. The other part was borrowed from artists such as James Brown, Charles Brown, Nappy Brown, and Gatemouth Brown. There were a lot of Browns in the blues world. Savoy Brown was simply added to that list.

As we drove through rush-hour traffic, I thought to myself of all the kings, queens, princes, princesses, and royalty, in general, from around the world who had frequented the Savoy and contributed to its immense history. Arriving on time, we found the rear entrance and unloaded our equipment. The hotel's imposing structure loomed overhead, casting shadows a century old. A doorman pointed the way inside, and we carried our gear into a large ballroom that seemed more appropriate for a classical music recital than a blues/rock show. Chandeliers hung from the ceiling. The light shining through the crystal illuminated a beautiful wood floor and sparkled on silver plates. Intimidated, I nevertheless set up my Vox AC 30 amplifier and waited apprehensively for our audience to arrive. I thought to myself, "Perhaps I'm in for a surprise. Maybe it'll be a young, hip crowd." I was thinking maybe this might be part of the debutante scene I occasionally played. A girl would see us at a club or college and be impressed enough to have us hired for a coming-out dance.

I was deluding myself. By nine o'clock, a cross section of the English aristocracy had seated themselves at tables surrounding the empty dance floor and awaited our performance. I walked onstage and nervously started playing. It was obvious someone had made a mistake! There were amazed looks on the faces of those sitting out front. After a few songs with Youlden belting out lyrics like "Squeeze my lemon, baby, till the juice runs down my leg" and me answering with howling guitar licks, a dignified elder lady walked up to the stage and spoke to bassist Bob Brunning.

"Could you please turn the noise down?" I heard her say.

Bob replied, "Do you mean turn down THE MUSIC?"

She fired back, "No, I said THE NOISE!" She wasn't so dignified now. Heated words were exchanged, and she returned to her seat. Somehow we continued on, and after finishing the show we made our exit back to the dressing room. We actually had gotten everyone onto the dance floor, but I'm sure the alcohol had more to do with that than our playing. Backstage, the conversation followed somewhere along these lines:

"Who booked the date?"

"I'll kill him!"

"Let's change agents tomorrow."

"We need a new manager."

"I'm quitting!"

It was finally decided that the hotel people, who had contacted our agency, must have been attracted to the name Savoy Brown, thinking the music would fit because of the similarity between the names. Harry, commission in mind, obviously did not want to disappoint anyone. That was the only scenario we could think of to pacify our frayed nerves. However, the hotel people disapproved and felt they had been misled or, possibly, duped. They decided the band was not going to be paid that night. Now, musicians can put up with almost anything, but nonpayment ranks as a capital crime. Needless to say, we were not happy. We therefore regrettably decided to take payment in kind. After everyone had left, as we were loading our van, we simply helped ourselves to some of the regal goodies that comprised the fixtures and fittings of the grand hotel, and handed them around.

It was not a very classy end to the night, but there was a feeling of vindication going around. After all, the conversation went, we were booked and had fulfilled our end of the transaction. It wasn't our fault! There were complaints from each party the next day. There were telephone calls between the manager, agent, group, and promoter. I can chuckle about it now, and although it was decades ago, the memory stays vivid in my mind. Eventually, silver ashtrays and such were returned, and the record was set straight. In the end, the whole mess blew over, although I'm still not sure if the band was ever paid.

# CHAPTER 10

## STOLEN GUITAR, FLYING V, AND BAND CHANGES

The only way that we can live is if we grow.
—C. JoyBell C.

After using my Fender Telecaster for so long, I decided I needed a change of equipment. Eric Clapton was part of the reason for the change. He had set his Telecaster aside and was playing a Gibson Les Paul. Mike Bloomfield, likewise, inspired by Clapton, also switched over to a Les Paul. Two of my biggest influences had changed their instruments. That was enough for me, and I followed suit. My next guitar was also a Gibson Les Paul. Mine wasn't the classic 1950s model but an early 1960s double-cutaway version later known as the SG model. It had the classic SG red-colored finish. It was more difficult for me to play with my small hands since it had a wide fretboard. Still, I was getting a much-fuller and heavier sound. The two built-in humbucker pickups gave the guitar a broader tone than my Telecaster. That sound was hard to control because it almost had a life of its own. It was like riding a wild horse that needed harnessing. I played many gigs with the guitar, but I was usually fighting the instrument. It was in control of me and not me of it. Then, while I was still learning how to control the guitar, it was stolen.

It may surprise many readers, but theft is a major problem when you're out on the road touring. A dressing room has to be secure. If not, you take everything onstage with you. You quickly learn about human failings when your bags or your coat or your guitars get stolen. It's all happened to me more than once. My SG was my first stolen guitar (there have been many). I remember being stoic about it. We had played a gig, somewhere, hours away from London. As usual, we drove home after the gig. We got to our homes quite late in the morning. Road manager Brian Wilcock dropped everyone off and, being so tired himself, went to bed, leaving the two guitars in the parked van. When he awoke, the van had been broken into, and the instruments were gone. He was heartbroken. I was in a fix.

Shortly thereafter, news came to us via Stan Webb, of the band Chicken Shack, that he had seen the guitars at a house. They were being sold privately. He had gone to check out the sale and realized they were our stolen guitars. Stan gave Harry the address and we both went along, with a driver, to somehow get the guitars back. It was a dark and rainy night typical of April weather. We drove to a street that wasn't in a bad area of the city. The houses were three stories high and had small front yards separated from the pavement by stone walls about 3 feet high. Harry told me to wait while he investigated. I was happy to stay in the car and avoid being involved in any confrontation. Time drifted by. I wasn't sure what Harry might accomplish, but I felt good knowing we were close to some kind of resolution. It must have been a good half-hour wait in the car. Suddenly in the rear mirror, I saw Harry running down the street toward the car, carrying two guitars, minus the cases, in his hands. He was yelling something, but I couldn't hear properly. He was agitated, and with good reason. There appeared, from the front door of the house, two men giving chase brandishing swords!

It was unbelievable! Harry jumped into the car with the guitars. I was happy. The two men chasing were not. They cursed and shouted as we sped away, and the two of us convulsed in nervous laughter. Harry told the story as we drove back home. He had, indeed, confronted the men, and after a conversation that was getting nowhere, he simply grabbed the guitars and took off, saying, "They're our guitars and you know it." When they produced the swords, he ran faster than a cheetah. Thus it was over, and I was reunited with my SG! Before the stolen guitars were recovered, I needed a guitar to play the gigs scheduled during that time. Harry didn't have enough money in the band account for me to buy a new guitar. Road manager Brian lent me the money, and he was happy to do so since he felt very guilty about leaving the stolen guitars unattended. I started looking around for a replacement. I walked into a music store and saw a Gibson Flying V displayed. The Flying V is a solid guitar that is, literally, shaped like an inverted V. I was aware of the guitar from seeing Lonnie Mack and Albert King using them. Dave Davies of the Kinks also used what I believe was the first model in the UK. I asked the salesman if I could buy the guitar.

"Peter Green wants it," he replied.

Peter Green had replaced Eric Clapton in John Mayall's band and was the new star player touring with John around the country.

I asked, "Has Peter put a holding deposit on the guitar?"

"No" was the answer.

That was all I needed to hear. I gave the salesman all the cash I had on me as an official deposit. I rushed home and got Brian's money and bought the V. That was the start of a beautiful relationship. The guitar, I was told, had been brought into the country by the Australian band The Easybeats. The instrument certainly wasn't being officially imported. It was too expensive, and there wasn't much of a market for it. The shape gave it a novelty guitar vibe, and I loved using it because of that. It poked a finger in the eye of those having a purist view of how a guitar should look. It had a tobacco sunburst finish and came with a whammy bar. It had a smaller neck that fit my small hands. The sound was pure blues. It just had that tone. All I had to do was choose the right amplifier. I didn't want what everyone else had, so I played through a Sound City amplifier at first. I tried a few other boutique models before giving in and buying a Marshall.

I ended up not being a "one-guitar guy." It was traveling in America that changed things. Instruments were so inexpensive in the 1960s if you looked in the right places. Those places were usually pawn shops. I found my Gibson Les Paul Junior, the one I played slide on "Tell Mama," in Minneapolis for fifty dollars. Guys out to make a buck would come to shows with guitars they had picked up at pawn shops and were trying to sell at a profit. They'd start the night asking a reasonable price, but I'd wait until load-out time after the show was finished, knowing they needed to make a sale. I was able to buy some classic vintage guitars for three hundred dollars or less. The most I paid was for a Gibson Black Beauty Les Paul. I sprung for nine hundred bucks for that one. It would cost you the price of a house these days.

I turned down lots of guitars that would now bring a small fortune. They were tools to me, and I was never a real collector anyway. Lots of musicians were collectors and still collect. On one occasion, Brian picked up a 1950s Flying V made of Korina wood, an extremely rare instrument now worth thousands. I played it but hated the big, chunky neck.

"Want it for a hundred dollars?" Brian asked.

"No thanks," I replied. "You keep it."

This period was the only time I had more guitars than I knew what to do with. I had them in attics, under beds, in basements, and even under my parents' beds! I came across great guitar deals as late as the 1990s. My drummer T. Xiques alerted me to a guitar in a pawn shop in Beaumont, Texas. Sure enough, there was an older 1970s Gibson 335 hanging on the wall. It was a steal at four hundred dollars. It has been fun buying guitars. Each one has a different characteristic and can make you play things you never thought you had in you. I have an Epiphone jazz box guitar at home. Every time I play it, a soulful jazz song comes out of me!

I was now a successful musician and able to afford to leave home. I rented a flat in Wandsworth on Battersea Park Road. During part of that time, Ten Years After keyboardist Chick Churchill stayed with me and helped with the rent. The apartment was an open invitation to people before I knew better. I walked into my bathroom once, and a girl was shooting up . . . you get the idea. At that time, I fancied myself as one of the "in crowd." An A-list drug dealer would come to the flat weekly after first servicing other prominent musicians. He would sell me some hashish, and I would roll it, with tobacco, into a smokable cigarette. I thought I was being cool and part of my group of peers.

That went on for a month or so until I came to my senses . . . after first losing those senses. Let me explain. Before there was enough money for a car to pick me up for gigs, I would meet the band at Charing Cross Station, and we would drive together from there. I would catch a bus to the train station. One morning, against my usual practice, I rolled a joint and smoked some of it before heading out to catch the bus. I stood waiting at the bus stop . . . and I waited . . . and I waited and waited. Then I came to my senses. I hadn't been standing at the bus stop at all. I was leaning against a lamppost several yards away from the stop. The buses had been coming and going, and, judging by the looks I was getting from passengers on one bus, they thought it was odd behavior. I was now very late for the band meeting, and I had to rush. Feeling very foolish, I arrived late but didn't miss the show. That taught me a lesson. I stopped thinking I could hang with the fast crowd.

It was at this time, with my Flying V guitar on my shoulder and Chris Youlden as the singer, that I took the band through what seemed like a million personnel changes. The changes through that year made the band notorious. I do believe that taking the band through those numerous lineups actually helped the music grow. However, I was alone in my thinking. Although no one blinks an eye these days at band changes, back then, in the UK, there was a significant value placed on bands that kept their original lineup.

John Mayall's former drummer, Hughie Flint, had a stint with the band. What a great guy he was in the band. He was a slender, wiry type and sported a classic beard that made him look like a cool jazz musician. I remember conversations with Hughie on many occasions as we drove back late at night from gigs. We never socialized, but we played so many gigs together that we got to know each other quite well. While we talked on those long after-gig drives, Chris Youlden would often be sleeping on the floor in the back of the van. There was only one driver's bench seat up front that three people could squeeze into. On one occasion, we saw another band broken down on the side of the road. It was the Nice, and I recognized one of the band members. Keith Emerson, the great Hammond organ player, was standing to one side trying to hitch a ride. We stopped and accommodated him. He climbed up front beside me on that driver's bench seat. The conversation was going great guns, and we were having a good time, when, from the back, I heard a band member shuffling.

"What's with all that talking. What's going on?" Chris grumpily said. "It's Keith Emerson, and we're giving him a lift home." I could hear the excitement in my voice because we had such a good musician in our midst. "Fucking pop star" was the reply, and my bandmate pulled the blanket back over his head. That killed the camaraderie instantly. There was an awkward silence for the rest of the drive back to London.

Bill Bruford, who later established himself as one of Britain's finest, was another drummer in the band. He was really accomplished but just wasn't a blues drummer. As good as he was, I had to fire him. He was very disappointed and really wanted to know why. I didn't know what to tell him. I didn't understand myself, only that he just wasn't a good fit. He would play too technically for what the music needed. I certainly didn't want to say something that would negatively influence him or stop his progression. I just mumbled that it wasn't working, and left it at that. Even he laughs at it all now.

Bob Brunning played bass for a while. He had started with Fleetwood Mac until John McVie finally took over. Bob later wrote a book on his experiences with the blues scene of the 1960s. It includes the story of how I returned to a hotel in Germany after being out on a date but was completely nonplussed with myself after discovering that my date was a man, or, should I say, transvestite? Now, that's a story that's very hazy in my mind. It's always interesting reminiscing with friends about events stretching back fifty years and more. They remember things I've long forgotten, and I remember things they have no memory of whatsoever.

Hughie Flint and Bob Brunning made up the rhythm section for a single we recorded in late 1967. The A side was "Taste and Try Before You Buy," the first solo song penned by Chris Youlden. The B side was my own composition, "Somewhere People." Youlden's song was largely missed by the public, most likely because it was way out in front of its time when it was released. The band personnel morphed for a while. I had certainly learned some lessons about musicians and made sure no other lead guitarist was brought into the group. Mostly, it was a revolving door of bass players and drummers. The year sped by, and it seemed as if I had played a million gigs. There was a University All-Night Carnival Rave with the Who. There were many return gigs at the Marquee, with acts such as Jethro Tull and Ten Years After opening the show. We played at the Boat Club in Nottingham, the Fishmongers Arms, London's Middle Earth (a venue for hippies), and a list of other venues that goes on and on. The band was still billed as the "Savoy Brown Blues Band" on many of the posters. The original apostrophe on the band's surname had, by now, been dropped. One of the strangest gigs occurred when the band and I played a private affair. I found myself being driven down a long private drive. The Scottish firs on either side were the tallest pines I had ever seen. We passed a guesthouse on my right that was bigger than any home I had ever lived in. The car rounded the final turn, and there, in front of me, was a house as big as a castle. We were to provide the music for a debutante at her coming-out dance. She had seen the band at college and wanted us for entertainment. We were ushered to the back of the building. I looked up at the gargoyles, and they seemed displeased at a blues band arriving under their noses. Our debutante host was lovely, and she showed us to the "stage" area. We set our gear up inside the large fireplace . . . it was that big. The only further recollection I have was eating at the splendid buffet and drinking copious amounts of champagne. Both of those will keep any musician happy. Hours later, after playing and driving back to London, Bob Hall and I stopped at our favorite all-night street-side pie stand. It must have been 2:00 a.m. by then. We ate our steak and kidney pies standing at the makeshift counter.

"This is the life," Bob said. "I love these pies, best in London." "Right you are," I replied. "They didn't have these on the buffet." Eventually the lineup started to stabilize following the addition of rhythm guitarist Dave Peverett. Dave was a few years older than me and closer to my brother's age. Dave was my brother's good friend, and I had befriended Dave's brother, John, who was closer to my age. I had seen Dave play with his own band and had even gone with him and his brother on a gig. I believe I may have played some guitar on that gig. I knew that Dave's band had disbanded, and he had gone to Switzerland for a period of time. When he returned to London, I asked him to join my band. I remember calling him up.

"Do you want to join Savoy Brown?" I asked.

He said, "That'd be great. Yes. When do you want me to start?" "Tonight" was my reply.

I could hear Dave's jaw drop at the other end of the line. He was surprised, to say the least.

"We'll be around this afternoon to pick you up," I confidently said. Dave always reminded me and told the story that within an hour of his saying yes, I had picked him up at his home and whisked him away for the first gig. He had no idea of the material, songs, or what was expected of him. That was me. I was fearless in my own musical risk-taking and drew everyone else along in that vortex. It all worked out, and Dave became a huge part of the lineup before eventually going on to form his own platinum-selling band, Foghat. Rivers Jobe was the next to enter the picture, on bass guitar. Rivers was about 5 foot 7 and of a slight build. He spoke with a refined London accent, and he played in the band for a good portion of 1968. I remember him always being slightly wary and suspicious of me. I assumed it was because of my leadership position. Later on in the year, we parted company. It is possible that Rivers came into the band via an open audition. I don't quite remember. I would often have open auditions in an attempt to fill positions. That is, we'd put an advertisement in the paper, announcing the band was auditioning for a particular musician. A hall would be hired, and a hundred musicians would turn up. It was madness looking back, but I've done many interesting things in attempts to fill open positions. For example, I once drove four hours to audition a drummer in HIS basement. At the mass auditions, each person would get a turn to play with the band. Of course, this achieved nothing. I often chose the wrong person. All sorts of wannabes showed up. A famous progressive-rock guitarist once told me he showed up at a Savoy Brown audition to be the harmonica player!

Open auditions, so often a waste of time, did produce drummer Roger Earl. Roger showed up with a double drum kit and a fabulous look. I had never seen a double drum kit before, and Roger played it like Ginger Baker. I was enthralled by his playing and image. He had it all down . . . jazz, rock, and blues. Roger sported a wonderful handlebar mustache. He was two years older than me, and he laughed a lot. He was self-deprecating, good looking, and long haired, with an air about him that he could handle a sword. He was a swashbuckler! He was given the gig, and I got that one right. Roger, too, went on to great fame with Foghat. Indeed, a one-time Savoy Brown lineup morphed itself into that band . . . minus yours truly. I was still on my own path.

Many of the musicians' names and faces escape me in the period of time from late 1967 into 1968. Some of them would laugh at me behind my back and even openly. They thought I was going nowhere. I was serious about something they took frivolously . . . music. I must admit my seriousness must have bordered on the boring.

Eventually, bassist Tony Stevens joined the band, but I do not recall how he came to my attention. Tony had a love of cars and drove a nice Citroën at the time. He brought a pleasant manner with him to the table. I have often thought that a person's demeanor was as important as how they play. I believe it was B.B. King who said, for his bands, it was "90 percent man and 10 percent musician." While deciding if I wanted Tony in the band, I recall sitting in his car and enjoying his company. For a start, he HAD a car, and I didn't. Tony was round faced, dark haired, and handsome. He had a touch of devilry mixed in with a youthful charm that was captivating. He was the kind of person you wanted to know more about, and I felt he had a solid enough personality to survive the rigors of the road life I would be leading him through. He played a Danelectro bass, which is an unusual instrument characterized by two long horns jutting out from the body of the guitar. His playing was complementary, and I could see he WAS a bass player and not someone who secretly wanted to be the guitar player (a failing that many bass players have). So, Tony had a car and good equipment. He was bringing something to the table. That's important to any relationship.

Finally, after many personnel changes, the band was once again as formidable a unit as the original lineup. It was now me on lead guitar, Dave Peverett on rhythm guitar, Chris Youlden on vocals, Tony Stevens on bass, and Roger Earl on drums. That was the band that first went to the United States, becoming a headliner and a hit chart act. It was a band that helped change the course of popular music. It was a band that brought joy to countless people, and that's the most important thing. It's odd that a music endeavor requiring total dedication, serious personal application, much inner anguish, and outside confrontation can result in bringing happiness to others' lives . . . but it does.

# CHAPTER 11

## *GETTING TO THE POINT*, *BLUE MATTER*, AND THE USA

Lead singers not only do the majority of the work, but their personalities are singled out and taken as the general attitude of the unit.

—Martha Reeves

It was 1968, and the violent anti–Vietnam War protests were going on in England, leading to clashes between protesters and the police. I didn't understand the war completely, but I certainly understood that the American soldiers, themselves, shouldn't be held in such contempt. I argued the fact with my brother and others. There was confusion in society, and I had my own ball of confusion in keeping a band intact. Somehow, that year I got to take the group into the studio to record the second and third albums.

The first album recorded that year was *Getting to the Point*. Just as we did for the first album, we went into Decca studios in West Hampstead. I had my Flying V guitar and a 50-watt Marshall amplifier. My sound had taken on a different texture. Whereas the first album was simply an album of covers, I began to write songs and fed Chris Youlden ideas that led to cowritten tunes. Nevertheless, I did include a couple of cover songs. One was a Willie Dixon song, "You Need Love," which many say served as a blueprint for Led Zeppelin's "Whole Lotta Love." I may be being fanciful, but I had, in fact, played a show that year with the Yardbirds, and Jimmy Page was on guitar. It was at a college, and there was no stage. Both bands set up and played on the floor. I was playing "You Need Love" as part of my set at the time. Page was playing the guitar with a violin bow, which I thought was unique. It was a technique he later brought to the world via Led Zeppelin.

*Getting to the Point* was a solid blues offering, but on the aforementioned track, "You Need Love," I took the music to a rock-edged approach again. Producer Mike Vernon got so annoyed with the deviation from straight blues that he walked out of the studio and left me to finish the track on my own! The UK album cover showed a photo of me wearing glasses that reflected the image of a Black man. The American release had a different album cover. It showed a maze that someone at the record company must have thought fit the title. I was, again, too busy gigging to even think about it. *Getting to the Point* was released in the USA, and again, I never listened to the final product. How could I? There were too many gigs to play on the calendar. I had little time to reflect.

*Blue Matter* was the second album recorded in 1968, and it was not released until 1969. It's the third album in the Savoy Brown catalog. One side was a live recording made on December 6 at the City of Leicester College of Education, while the other side of the album consists of studio material. Singer Chris Youlden decided he wasn't feeling good enough to make the live show. That didn't sit too well with me, Mike Vernon, or the rest of the band members. I simply had rhythm guitarist Dave Peverett sing the songs instead of Chris. Dave had lots of singing experiences with his own band prior to joining me, but he was still nervous. The performance itself was touch and go. At a later date, we went into the studio and recut Dave's vocals, but on that night, some of my best guitar playing ever was captured. Upon the album's release, one of the live songs, "Louisiana Blues," became an underground hit in the USA.

The studio side of *Blue Matter* featured one of the band's best songs ever. Even *Rolling Stone* magazine recognized "Train to Nowhere" as the "quintessential Savoy Brown song." I think it was the only time *Rolling Stone* gave the band any positive consideration at all. It was a simple concept that I had for the song. I set out to write a tune in the fashion of the Junior Parker song "Mystery Train," which had been made famous by Elvis Presley. I had the music and title, and I gave the idea to Chris Youlden for him to write the lyrics. Rivers Jobe was the bass player. Rivers lived in Mayfair and had received an education at the exclusive Charterhouse School. He certainly had a different background than most other musicians at the time. He later went on to a career in progressive rock. He cultivated a rock star look, with long hair covering one eye. During the session, he already had progressive ideas. When I asked him to play the two simple notes on the intro, he fought me over it. We clashed over the simple part, but he eventually played the part. I interpreted Rivers's attitude as an inability to be a team player. Following a few other incidents a short time later, I replaced him in the band with Tony Stevens. Producer Mike Vernon came up with the horn ideas on "Train to Nowhere," which gave it such a final unique touch and feel.

On the track "Don't Turn Me from Your Door," I encouraged Youlden to play guitar himself. I even gave him one of my guitars as a gift. It was a new white Burns solid electric guitar. His primitive style suited the song beautifully. He played the part more authentically than I could.

America seemed a long way off in late 1968. The UK blues boom of 1968 was fading. Blues had become a bandwagon that hundreds of bands had jumped on. That bandwagon broke under the weight. The bands that best exemplified the blues during the boom years were my own, John Mayall and his Blues Breakers, Fleetwood Mac, and Chicken Shack. The two latter groups had commercial hit records on the British charts. I, with Savoy Brown, had none. Without a hit, it was difficult to grow. I told Chris Youlden we had about two years left as a band.

In the meantime, brother Harry was working in an office with Terry Ellis and Chris Wright. Harry was managing Savoy Brown, while Terry Ellis managed and booked Jethro Tull. Chris Wright managed and booked Ten Years After. That conglomeration, essentially, was the beginning of what would become the Chrysalis company. Jethro Tull and Ten Years After had already been to the United States and had toured successfully. Dee Anthony was being used as the American representative and facilitator to enable the acts to enter the USA. It was arranged for him to come to England to check out my band. It was going to be my turn with Savoy Brown.

Harry and I were nervous before that meeting because singer Chris Youlden had a very unorthodox look onstage. He was tall, thin, gangly, and hunched over. His complexion was gray, and he always carried a look that was not quite shifty but always on guard. His brownish hair was wispy. His blues voice was unmatched in authenticity, and I cared little about his appearance. However, would his appearance be seen as a challenge for Dee Anthony and the American market to absorb? Harry decided to spruce Chris up. After all, he was the front man, and singers tended to sell the band's music as well as themselves. Harry bought a long fur coat that diverted the attention away from Chris's hunch, and it also gave him an eccentricity that matched his personality. We were all nervous the night Anthony came to a club to see us perform. Could we rely on Chris? He would be the main focus. Chris was brilliant that night, and Dee was only too happy to bring the band to the USA. We would follow our stablemates, Jethro Tull and Ten Years After, in addition to all the other British acts that had paved the way, from the Beatles to Cream. There were visa problems to overcome before the band could work in the USA. Once they were sorted out, and it was all last minute, I found myself on a transatlantic flight. The entire band did their best to get a view out of the airplane windows as we were approaching New York City. We had our first glimpse of the city's skyscrapers and what we were hoping was going to be a new lease on life. It was January 1969 when I first landed in New York City for my first American tour. I was the next wave of bringing the blues back to America, where blues music had been born. I was well aware, even at that late time, that blues music was undervalued, and the great artists of the genre were totally unknown to the mainstream public. I felt I could help change that. I could bring the blues to a new generation of kids and awaken them to musicians they were not aware of.

In fact, like those 1960s British musicians before me, I was on a mission. We played a show in New York City the very first night we arrived on January 24. It was at Steve Paul's venue called the Scene Club. On January 18, we had played at Mothers, a club in Birmingham in the UK, so there wasn't much time to deliberate before heading across the Atlantic. We didn't have our normal stage equipment with us when we arrived in New York, and we were provided with the back line (amplifiers and drums). It was horrendous. We were exhausted. The club was full of fellow musicians, and I considered the performance a total embarrassment. Harry was there, and he kept telling road manager Brian to have the band turn down the volume. We were louder than thunder. I did go back to the club, as an onlooker, many times after that because it was open late and featured many great up-and-coming acts. I saw Sha Na Na there as well as Rick Derringer with a version of his band the McCoys. But I still shudder thinking of my first American performance.

Another New York City venue we played a few times was Ungano's. The owner was great and made us feel at home. I don't have much recollection of the band's or my own performances there. I probably played with my head down and a feeling of dread. Playing onstage isn't all it's cracked up to be. Often, when you're younger and even now, you're concerned about audience reaction. I also frequented Ungano's as an audience member. It was a great club for national acts that were just starting up, or older acts that were experimenting. I saw Van Morrison and the Tony Williams Lifetime there. The latter act featured John McLaughlin, the great British jazz guitarist. I already had a record by John at the time, and it was a pure jazz offering. I was nonplussed when I saw him playing onstage with Williams. He had a Gibson Les Paul Junior, and he was playing through a full Marshall stack. He seemed to have no control over the huge rock/blues sound . . . a sound I helped pioneer in England two years earlier. But I could see he was making an artistic statement, and I loved the band.

I do have a memory of jamming at Ungano's. Chris Youlden and I went to see blues and R&B singer Bobby Bland perform there. Someone then arranged for Chris and myself to get onstage and jam with Bland and his band. We did a slow blues. I played an introduction, and Bobby started singing a verse or two.

Then he started to "scat" sing a verse . . . a main feature of his style. He then handed the microphone to Chris. I could see a slight smile of victory on Bland's face that seemed to say, "Beat that." Little did Bobby know, but scat singing was also a strong part of Youlden's vocal repertoire. Chris sang amazingly. Bobby Bland's jaw dropped to the floor. I had never quite understood that phrase until that night. We were triumphant; well, certainly Chris had been. We had held our own with one of the greatest blues and R&B singers the world has ever seen.

# CHAPTER 12

## NEW YORK, BIG CITIES, AND JAMMING WITH THE BEST

Toil without song is like a weary journey
without an end.
—H. P. Lovecraft

New York City played a huge role in my life when I first arrived in the United States. Playing those clubs was important, and it was marvelous just taking in the atmosphere. At first, I dressed as I would back in England . . . velvet pants, snappy flowered shirts, and snakeskin boots. I quickly found out, by walking around Midtown dressed that way, that I was going to draw the wrong human element my way. Within hours of my first day in the city, I was wearing jeans and a white T-shirt. I fit in much better that way. I thought I was completely incognito, but avid concertgoers still recognized me from shows and would say nice things as they passed.

Long Island, just east of New York City, also played a pivotal role in my development. I played in many clubs on Long Island. At one of the gigs, a large contingent of tough and gang-like bikers showed up. I had only read about biker gangs like them before. The night ended abruptly when a fight started in front of the stage, and they decided to involve the band. We ran out the back and made a quick escape.

The first time touring the US was a learning experience for all of us. After one gig, Brian was driving the band back to the hotel and was pulled over by a patrol car for a minor infraction. He didn't have his driver's license with him and realized he had left it at the hotel. There would be no excuses. He was taken then and there by the police officers and put in jail overnight. I had to drive to pick him up the next morning and pay the fine. We had to learn fast.

We were based in New York City quite a bit during the first tour, and I visited the Apollo Theater in Harlem with Brian. We saw the Chi-Lites perform. We weren't sure of how we would be received in an all-Black community, so we arrived late, sat in the back, and left early. We had a great time, and the young Black girls my age caught my eye, but that wasn't the time to go a-courting. At a later date, I jammed at a Harlem club with the jazz Hammond organist Lonnie Smith. It was one of my more successful sit-ins. The club was incredibly tiny and was more of a corner bar. I crammed in next to Lonnie on a postage-stamp-sized stage and played off that wonderful Hammond sound. It really is a pleasure for a guitarist to play along with the classic organ sound. It's a perfect compliment.

In New York the band always stayed at the Loew's Midtown Hotel. In fact, it's where a lot of bands were booked. I was amazed at the quality of the hotel room. It was much nicer than any I normally stayed in throughout Europe. It was even nicer than my own home. The hotel was populated by tourists, but after midnight, hookers were always hanging around. Down the road from the hotel was a bar where we'd all hang out at night. The groupies soon found that out, and it was playtime for a lot of musicians. I ran into Robert Plant outside the Loew's. Led Zeppelin was already tearing up the popularity charts. He gave me some advice. "Put on a show for the audience and wiggle your ass if the music isn't doing the trick," he chuckled. "And start listening to Moby Grape; they are great." I was happy just to have him talk to me. I took his advice to heart, and I was soon the proud owner of a Moby Grape album.

I was soon involved with a lady named Madeline, and she became my first wife. I very crazily took her back to England and bought my first home with her. It was a cedar-built ranch-style home in Sussex, a long way from London. I was going to be a country gent. The marriage ended very quickly, and it cost me a lot of money in addition to the new country home I had bought. I was starting to live too fast. I had no guidance or close friends. I was on my own to make all the mistakes a young man with too much attention, too much talent, too much ego, and too little common sense could make.

One of my major problems was the inability to live alone. For someone who calls himself a loner, I know that's an oxymoron. What I'm saying is I couldn't live without a female relationship. I needed that comfort. I wanted a homelife. It was too depressing having the great lifestyle I did without someone to share it with. It's bad enough going to an empty hotel room each night after a gig where people were clapping for you and putting you on a pedestal. However, going home to an empty home, after three months of intense work, life experience, and celebrity, was worse. I should have worked it out more and been mature, but the fact is that I was quite immature throughout those years.

Using New York City as a base, the band started to expand to other cities. Boston was close at hand, and I played at the Boston Tea Party with the J. Geils Band as the opening act. The next day, Peter Wolf took Dave and me to the local record stores, which we greatly appreciated. It was the beginning of our tendency to load suitcases with new albums. Peter was different from anyone I had met before. He had an edgy street vibe that I now understand but couldn't relate to at the time.

We went to Chicago and played the Kinetic Playground with Blood, Sweat and Tears, and it served as an introduction to the city that was the birthplace of my musical style. I also seem to recall another gig at the same time in Old Town, Chicago. It was with the band Chicago, but perhaps that's all a dream. I know for certain these days that I can't say I haven't played a town or city, because someone will contradict me and say I was somewhere in such and such a year. The gigs and towns blend together as in an Alfred Hitchcock movie flashback. I do remember, for sure, playing the Kinetic Playground again later that year, with Led Zeppelin as the headliner, Jethro Tull as the special guest, and Savoy Brown as second on the bill, following an opening act. During sound check, I jammed with John Bonham on drums. Ian Anderson joined in on flute. Backstage, I was offhand with Robert Plant because someone said he had gone out with my girlfriend. I was miffed. He had no idea why I was being so antisocial.

There was also an interesting incident that took place in those early days in Chicago. I decided, with Brian, to visit the Pepper's Lounge, a blues club in South Chicago. The aftermath of the 1968 race riots had become a factor in the city, but that was something we weren't quite aware of. Brian and I drove to the club in a rental car. The South Side neighborhood was a Blacks-only area. I guess it was called a ghetto back then. I had a glamorous image of what to expect. European magazines tended to view the gritty world of blues through rose-colored glasses and wrote about how safe such visits were. We got lost and stopped by a parked police squad car. They gave us directions, and we had no problems getting to the club. We parked and walked in along a hallway to see a bandstand to my left. A band was playing, and the bar faced the stage. In front, and to my right, were benches. Everyone turned and looked. It was obvious from the moment we made eye contact that we were in the wrong place at the wrong time. We sat on the benches feeling a little out of place, to put it mildly. There had been much social rioting going on around Chicago in those days, in addition to Blacks and whites being involved in racial disputes.

Segregation was still fresh in people's minds. We had committed a major faux pas. At that moment, when it seemed the band had stopped playing and the atmosphere was closing in on us, through the front door and down the hallway came the two policemen who had given us directions. They took us by the arm and escorted us back to the car. They politely explained that the area could be dangerous, and, if we had stayed, trouble may have followed. I thanked them and drove back to my own world . . . a world far removed from a South Side Chicago blues bar.

On my first trip down south, to the state of Georgia, the band opened for Little Richard in a theater. After the show, Richard said he was going to a local club to see B.B. King play. Dave Peverett and I joined the retinue of people tagging along with him. The audience at the venue was all Black, and we seated ourselves, with Richard, at the back of the hall behind picnic tables. Throughout the night, Little Richard signed autographs. The dance floor was full of couples slow-dancing to songs such as "Three O'Clock Blues." Someone must have told B.B. King that Dave and I were there with Richard. From the stage, he said, "We have a British band with us here tonight. Give them a big hand. I'm told they're Britain's answer to the Supremes!" Now that was good for a laugh. I was too shy to go backstage and say hello, and I certainly didn't want to embarrass B.B. by telling him he had been given the wrong information!

It was that same year that I was in Los Angeles and heard that guitarist Albert Collins had a residency at a local bar. Again, with Dave in tow, I went to see his act. Albert was mostly an instrumentalist at that time, and his playing sent me into a crazy frenzy. Dave and I were on our feet and clapping. Believe it or not, the audience numbered only about twelve, and most of the tables were empty. I kept returning to the club and spoke with Albert a little. One night, I got onstage to jam with him. Another guitar player joined us. It was Earl Hooker! Hooker was the sensational slide guitar player who turned my life around when I heard his playing on the Muddy Waters song "You Shook Me." That was the song that inspired me to concentrate on a Chicago blues style. So, there I was mixing it up onstage with two of the greatest guitar players in the world, and two of my idols . . . Albert Collins and Earl Hooker!

You can see why I look back at 1969 so fondly. At another Los Angeles club, I was sitting and watching a local band play. In those days, I'd play a night or two at a concert, and the rest of the week I'd have free time. That night, I was nursing a beer and enjoying the L.A. nightlife. Out of nowhere, Jimi Hendrix walked onstage, took a guitar from one of the guitar players, and started to jam with the band. This was too good an opportunity to miss. I, too, got onstage, grabbing the other guitar player's instrument. Jimi and I went back and forth with guitar licks. Before I knew it, we were joined by singer Eric Burdon, who proceeded to light up the club with his great voice. Afterward, I joined Jimi at his table . . . he was living in L.A. at the time. He struck me as being very humble, and that impression has stayed with me my whole life. I saw Jimi one time after that in a New York City club he was playing. It was a special occasion of some kind, perhaps an opening night. It was a time of personal turmoil for him, and his guitar playing was magnificent through a mixture of blues, rock, and gospel. I simply sat that night mesmerized in the audience. However, I got the feeling, at least in my mind, that he was troubled. It wasn't long after that he died from an accidental drug overdose.

# CHAPTER 13

## TOURING THE USA, DETROIT, AND CHRIS LEAVES THE BAND

I'm going down in Louisiana, baby behind the sun.
—Muddy Waters

I played many shows at the Fillmore East Auditorium. I think my first show was in February 1969, on the bill with headliner Chuck Berry and Johnny Winter . . . quite the bill. I watched the performance of Johnny Winter since he was just coming on the scene. He was excellent and a wild-looking guy with his pale features. The legend was already growing around him, and his albino status made that even more interesting. I sat through his show from a seat in the theater, a practice I often had when other bands on the bill interested me . . . and most of them did.

That year, we opened shows at the Fillmore or were special guests to acts such as the Grateful Dead; Blood, Sweat & Tears; and the Butterfield Blues Band. Some jokester said he thought we were the house band. By February 1970, the band was headlining at the Fillmore East. Nothing felt better than being under the spotlight on the Fillmore stage. The Fillmore audiences seemed like they all were aficionados, and I felt that each note I played was being absorbed and understood. By this time, Chris Youlden had perfected his onstage persona. He now had an even-longer fur coat and a top hat and smoked a long stogie onstage. He looked like a cross between a hobo and a menacing no-nonsense street guy. Harry kept working on Chris with his appearance. It was manufactured, but it suited the moment. The music and Chris's appearance forever etched a memory in the minds of fans across the country. A modern-day version of Chris's look even showed up wittingly, or unwittingly, with Slash of Guns 'n Roses fame. I don't think Chris was completely comfortable with his onstage look. He had to be coaxed and encouraged, and that was something Harry was great at doing.

At the Fillmore East, we'd play two shows each night, and there was a lengthy break between shows. I would go to Ratner's, a Jewish restaurant next door, after the first show and spend as much time as possible eating and talking. I was simply killing time. One night, I returned for the second show to find Harry and Chris passed out on the floor about forty-five minutes before showtime. The floor was soddened with water that had seeped out from the ice-filled drinks bin. I woke them up and the show went on, but not without some trepidation. Chris was great, as usual, but I think Harry slept through half the show.

Bill Graham, the Fillmore promoter, took a liking to us, and we continued our headline status with his encouragement. Graham ran the shows in a very professional manner. Everyone had to be on time and respect the venue's equipment. He didn't like microphones being broken or microphone stands being thrown around. He admonished one opening act from England that had a prepunk attitude. He warned them about throwing the microphones. The singer didn't listen. During that band's show, he tossed the microphone offstage into the wings . . . right into Bill! That act never worked the Fillmore again and never did catch on in America.

It took about a year to achieve top-of-the-bill status in America. During that year, the band played all over the country. We flew to the venues all the time, as did our equipment. Sometimes there were three flights a day. We'd be on the first flight every morning and catch up with an afternoon nap at our destination. I hardly ever got back home to London. I shared a room with Dave Peverett on the road or, occasionally, Tony Stevens. Tony kept a running log of the encores we would get. This was at a time when encores weren't necessarily forthcoming, especially for lower-on-the-bill bands. The band was growing and making an impact nationally. I never realized how well we were doing, apart from Tony's log, because I was contained in a "bubble." It was just me, the band, and a few handlers moving from city to city, hotel to hotel, and venue to venue.

The city of Detroit was a turning point in the band's success. In 1969 we must have played there, or in the general vicinity, a dozen times! The Grande Ballroom and the Eastown Theater were two of the venues that were pivotal in providing a foundation for the band to build upon. The Detroit audience loved Savoy Brown, and once we knew we were getting that attention, we wanted to capitalize on it to further our careers. I really felt that I didn't play to my full potential until I got on the Grande Ballroom stage. The audience made me come out of my shell. I was very shy. In fact, when I first started touring, I would often try to hide behind my amplifier onstage! Now, with a screaming crowd in front of me and a belly full of whiskey, I was playing the guitar as if my life depended on it. I started drinking more alcohol to help "charge" me up for a show and to get rid of my inhibitions. It worked, but I already had some issues handling booze, and those issues finally brought me to a place as low as you can go . . . but why spoil a good story so soon?!

The show's set list, at this time, consisted of songs mostly from the albums *Getting to the Point* and *Blue Matter*. Harry said it was the best set list ever.

Staples included "Louisiana Blues," "Train to Nowhere," "Honey Bee," and the "Savoy Brown Boogie." Originally, while touring in England, I had the band open the night with the Boogie. Harry told me I had it all wrong, and the Boogie should be the show closer. I did as he suggested, and the arrangement grew and grew as we continued to use it as the closer. In fact, when Savoy Brown's third album, *A Step Further*, was recorded in 1969, a live version of the "Savoy Brown Boogie" took up one full side! As the Boogie expanded, everyone had ideas of how to make it more memorable. Harry decided, before one of the Grande Ballroom shows in Detroit, that we should include a 1950s rock-and-roll medley somewhere in the middle of the song. I was upset for two reasons. I resented my brother's influence, and I didn't think a medley was appropriate. I hadn't come thousands of miles to play a rock-and-roll medley, and I let Harry know that in the dressing room backstage. He attacked back, and I was almost in tears. He finally won the argument, and I played the medley. Harry was right. It was just what was needed. Again, my purist attitude had gotten in the way.

We did not have a title for *A Step Further*, our second album in 1969, as it was nearing completion. However, one day, I went to the office of Walt McQuire, the A&R man at London Records in New York City. Walt had been around since the 1940s in music and came from a big-band tradition. He knew music inside and out. He had seen it all. He was a wonderful guy, a good guy, and a guy who didn't bullshit you. I was happy to call him a friend. He enjoyed life, liked a drink or two, and always had a smile on his face.

"Tell me about the record," he said.

"Well, we're taking things a step further," I started to explain.

"That's it," he exclaimed. "There's your album title."

*A Step Further* it was. The album took its title from the fact that we were now progressing within the blues musical framework. It would be the last album with Mike Vernon producing.

The epic version of the "Savoy Brown Boogie" that takes up an entire side of the album was recorded live at the Cooks Ferry Inn venue in Edmonton, England. Many, many years later, a fan who was at the show said he spoke to me that night and asked me, "How does one get so good at playing guitar?" He told me my answer was "Practice, practice, and practice."

The first side of the album featured three Chris Youlden songs and an instrumental composition that I had written. Chris, with Harry's encouragement, had started to write songs and had gotten very good at it. Chris would bring me the songs, and I'd arrange them before presenting them to the band. I was the go-between, and it worked well until my enthusiasm for Chris started to fade. As the relationship started to fracture, I heard, behind the scenes, that Chris had no love for me. I'm sure one of the things he didn't like was having to sit offstage while I played twenty-minute guitar solos. You might notice there are very few guitar solos on the subsequent Youlden solo albums. Chris had always had a somewhat curmudgeonly demeanor, and it showed in his songs in a poetic way. It made the material hard and edgy. "I'm Tired" was a classic take by Youlden on his dissatisfaction with the world around him. I was always able to echo Youlden's sentiments on guitar with call and response or by simply playing a sympathetic solo. Backing up a vocalist in that way has been something I've enjoyed immensely over the years.

Socializing with Chris was a very rare event. We met onstage and went our separate ways offstage. In truth, that could be said about almost all the band members. Everyone had their own way to enjoy themselves away from the shows. If I got together with any of the band members, it was Dave Peverett. Dave was tall and lanky and had a pale complexion. He had worn prescription black-rimmed glasses, in the style of Buddy Holly, when he was younger. He told me his eyesight improved when he stopped wearing glasses, and he hadn't needed them since. He was a thoroughly easygoing person who, like me, was a record and book collector. That brought us together. First and foremost, we were fans of the music. He had great respect for me and Chris and was the ultimate "team player." We all were enjoying life and happy to have separate lives away from the stress of playing gigs and traveling. *A Step Further* climbed up the Billboard charts to reach #71. We had broken into the Hot 100 for the first time. Things were looking up, and the gigs rolled on.

One of those gigs was at the Philadelphia Spectrum. It had a revolving stage that scared me, if I'm being truthful. Sly and the Family Stone were the headline band that night. Sly looked approachable backstage, but apart from a smile, I didn't pursue a conversation. Sometimes that is the best course of action. You just never know the state of mind of fellow artists, and I've often had to deal with rude and unsociable musicians while trying to be friendly. So, I was apprehensive. I can't remember doing a sound check. All I remember was being onstage playing the thirty-minute set. I'd look up and engage in eye contact with those in front of me. Then, a minute later, I'd look up and it was a brand-new audience! The revolving stage brought a new audience in front of me every few minutes. In addition, when I really looked up, I couldn't see into the upper levels, where so many people were seated. I had never played in such a large building in my life. I was unnerved by the whole experience. I much preferred being seated in the audience, later, watching Sly tear it up.

At the Fillmore West in San Francisco, it seemed the band was a headliner from the first show on. I remember watching other acts on the bill . . . Ry Cooder once and Humble Pie another time. I can't bring to mind much about my own performances at all. The venue was a building on the corner of South Van Ness Avenue and Market Street. I always thought it had a cold feeling inside. Really, it was just a large room with hard floors. It started as a swing-era dance hall, and I could easily imagine dancers doing the Lindy Hop. When I played, everyone sat on the floor and listened while the smell of marijuana wafted through the air. A few crazed people would be standing and swinging their arms around in a dance form I knew wasn't the Charleston.

The Winterland Ballroom was another San Francisco venue. The band opened for Janis Joplin in the winter of 1969, and I got my first taste of tequila that night. Everyone was drinking it and doing the whole salt-and-lemon-chaser routine while going on about the "worm in the bottom of the bottle." Janis became infatuated with Tony Stevens. I was sharing a room with Tony on that occasion and turned a blind eye to any physicality between the two of them. Tony was a ladies' man, and Janis was a passing ship. She tried to hang on to him, but it came to nothing.

That show with Joplin had been the first time the band had made it to the West Coast to gig. It had already been a two-month tour on the road. We played some concerts in the Los Angeles area and then also headlined for a few days at the Whisky a Go Go on Sunset Boulevard in West Hollywood. Delaney and Bonnie were on the bill along with the Aynsley Dunbar Retaliation. I also met the GTOs, and Miss Christine became a good friend. She's the one on the Frank Zappa *Hot Rats* album cover climbing out of the swimming pool. It was a purely platonic friendship. We went to art theaters together, and she was great company taking me around the city and simply hanging out. I saw her in London sometime after that, when she was there with Todd Rundgren, when she invited me to their apartment. We exchanged a little conversation, but Todd wasn't in the mood to socialize, and I took a quick leave.

I always thought of Christine, and decades later, when the internet came around, I did a quick search on her and found that she had died in 1972 of an overdose at age twenty-two. I was, and still am, saddened by her passing so young.

Cynthia "Plaster Caster" Albritton also came around to the Landmark hotel, where we often stayed while in Los Angeles. She was already a famous groupie by the time I met her. She liked to make plaster casts of musicians' erect penises. I declined the offer. The whole thing was too weird, but Tony Stevens went ahead and was immortalized in a mold!

My first time playing in a football stadium was interesting in that there was a riot going on outside. Ike and Tina Turner were headlining, and the whole bill was full of great artists. Fans outside were trying to get in, perhaps without paying, and there was a battle between them and the police. The promoter took me to the upper tier, and we were able to see the whole thing going on below us.

The fans were trying to break down the fences. The police were there in numbers, pushing them back. It was like watching a newsreel. For the show, I had my imported English equipment, a Marshall amplifier full stack. For the entire set, tour manager Brian was forced to stay behind the amplifier to continually replace blown fuses every few minutes. We had our own transformers with us because of the difference in the electrical wattage . . . 110 V in the US versus 240 V in Britain. It gave us all sorts of problems doing shows, and on that day for sure. A dozen fuses later, we had somehow gotten through the set!

The whole year was a back and forth between touring the US and playing gigs in the UK. While back home in London, we played a co-bill show at the Albert Hall with Jethro Tull. Terry Reid, starting a very promising career, was also on the bill. This is a show I'll never forget, and I'll tell you why. The afternoon before the appearance, I showed up at my brother's house to find out that musicians from the original Fleetwood Mac, including Peter Green, were there. They were smoking a spliff and passing it around. I didn't smoke, but I felt peer pressure on this occasion and joined in. Little did I know the joint was laced with some sort of hallucinogenic drug. I became completely stoned in a matter of minutes. A car arrived and took me straight to the venue. I was due to go onstage at 8:00 p.m. At 7:00 p.m., I was still out of my head! I somehow got onstage, and my guitar strings felt like spaghetti under my fingers. I was in a state of paranoia. I played the show and can only imagine I got through it on what you might call "automatic pilot." Back in the dressing room, I was full of relief, but now, in my hallucinogenic state, I was laughing uncontrollably. At that point, the night's guests walked in . . . my parents! I have no idea what they made of me. I was obviously not in control, and I tried to avoid them as much as possible. The night ended, and though many years went by after that, my mother and father never spoke of that gig to me ever again!

In that same year, Chris Youlden came to me with a group of songs he had written. It was one of those times I was staying with my parents in Tolworth, South London. Chris came to visit and set up in the front living room, playing an electric guitar without amplification. I placed my head close to the guitar to hear the chords, and he played me the new songs he had written. I loved them at first listen and brought them to the band. The songs became the body of work that would become the next Savoy Brown album, *Raw Sienna*. One of them, "Needle and Spoon," dealt with the drug heroin and looked at its use through the eyes of a user. Chris sang it in the first person even though he was not a drug user himself. He was skittish about doing the song because of its content. However, the last verse of the song is the warning "If you're married to H, you're married for life."

"That's enough to scare people away from the drug," I said optimistically. "Let's do it."

I tried to encourage Chris to sing it at live shows, but we never did, even when I suggested he do it alone on guitar. Chris and I also came up with the horn parts on the songs with Terry Noonan, and Terry transcribed our ideas. On those songs, I fingered the chords, and Terry literally wrote the music, per my finger positions, to get the correct voicing.

*Raw Sienna* was a wonderful collection of Youlden songs, but the album fared poorly. It reached #121 and did not crack the Hot 100 album chart. The live shows were also starting to suffer. I was playing lengthy guitar solos, and Chris was presenting himself as a sophisticated R&B singer. I lost belief in him and found the relationship between us a one-way street. A change was coming.

After *Raw Sienna* underperformed, Harry thought that another record label might be necessary. He went to Atlantic Records. They had always thought Savoy Brown was a Black band, and they wanted to sign us. Harry also went to Warner Brothers, and they, too, wanted to sign the band. Warner Brothers offered a huge advance with extra perks such as cars and houses thrown in. At this point in the negotiations with the other labels, Chris decided to leave the band, and everything fell flat. Harry and I went to the band with the idea that we would stay with Decca Records, and it was received favorably. We stayed with Decca (London Records).

Chris soon left the band for a solo career, and I wasn't at all unhappy to see him leave. I had some of my own songs written, and I was confident that Dave could take over the lead vocalist position while still playing rhythm guitar. He himself was a little less certain of that. After all, he was filling Chris's shoes, a big task. However, it was a task I knew he was capable of doing, and I wrote songs in carefully chosen keys while keeping Dave's voice in mind. Dave sang very differently than Chris, and I knew there would be no comparisons made in that way.

I was very confident in this time period. I had survived many band personnel changes and the criticisms that came with those changes. I survived being sacked from my own band and put myself in the minds and hearts of audiences as one of the best blues/rock guitarists on the planet. That confidence was going to keep me riding high for quite some time.

# CHAPTER 14

## LOOKING IN FROM THE OUTSIDE, AND THE SHOW MUST GO ON

You can do anything in this world if you are prepared to take the consequences.

—W. Somerset Maugham

Chris Youlden left the band in the winter of 1970 to continue onward with a solo career. I had been dominating the live shows as a guitarist, and Chris had become very unhappy with me and his role in the band. We had no communication together and saw one another only onstage or while we were traveling. I had lost my enthusiasm for him, and it just did not seem as if the band could go on productively with him as a member. He seemed very antisocial and uncommunicative. There was no love lost between us when he quit. It was a shame, because Warner Brothers wanted to sign the band with Chris as the singer, and that whole business idea never materialized. That really was a crossroads for the band at the time. We were, possibly, on the verge of superstardom, but it was not meant to be. Perhaps the whole idea was overreaching in the first place. Either way, the more modest career I have had since that junction has been more than enough for me to handle.

After a year of touring North America, I had now moved on to the new band configuration. My relationship with Decca Records continued, and the band was now a four-piece. I did not participate in any of the business decisions. Those all were backroom happenings overseen and controlled by Harry. Staying with Decca Records was a conservative position to take.

The Rolling Stones had left the company during this time period, and I was not thrilled to be staying. The absolute head of Decca Records, the man who founded the company in 1929, Sir Edward Lewis, did call me to ask why I was so unhappy with the company. I couldn't give him a definitive answer other than I didn't feel I was in a progressive environment.

Chris's leaving the band did not make me feel at all uncomfortable, because I had new material already written and ready to go. It would eventually make up the next album. Harry also knew it was good business ahead for him. He could now manage two artists, Chris and myself. Both of us were good prospects. I moved Dave Peverett into the lead singer position and wrote songs for his voice and talent. The band was now based around his vocals and my guitar playing, as Roger and Tony continued to hold down the rhythm section. It was the same band minus Chris Youlden as the front man. The change didn't stop the creative flow, and I was soon in the studio recording the sixth album, *Looking In*.

I started rehearsing the new song material with "Lonesome" Dave Peverett, Roger Earl, and Tony Stevens. I picked the right keys for Dave's voice so that he would be seen in the best light while moving the band forward. I was at the height of my young powers as a bandleader and musician. There was a momentum built up from the very beginning, a wave of destiny that I was riding. I was unaware of how privileged a position I was in. I had the whole ball of success in my hand, and I was running with it.

It was 1970, and the new decade had begun. It was going to be the era of the Boeing 747 jet airliner; a plane I would fly many times crisscrossing the Atlantic Ocean. In that same year, Paul McCartney left the Beatles, Black Sabbath released their first album, and Jimi Hendrix died. The music scene was changing. I felt the future was mine to mold in whatever fashion I desired.

Just as I had done on the *Raw Sienna* album, I took on the role of producer on the sixth album, *Looking In*, and decided it would be recorded at Recording Sound Studio in London. Paul Tregurtha was the engineer, and we worked well together. I had taken on quite a bit as the primary songwriter, guitar player, and producer. However, Tony Stevens wrote a couple of great songs that really helped enormously. My song "Looking In" was chosen as the title of the album. It was a philosophical song about looking in at life from the outside, not knowing the answers to life and wondering about what the future held. The album cover, a fantasy piece of artwork with a tinge of the horror genre, was done by Jim Baikie, an artist friend of Dave's. The logo on the front cover of *Looking In* is still in use today.

The recording went smoothly. During the process, I did have some misgivings about some of the songs, Dave's singing, and my playing. However, I kept those thoughts to myself. I always have misgivings about a new album. I also have a tendency not to play the guitar as hard as I can or should. I tend to lay back. On one track, "Leaving Again," the road crew taunted me to pull out all the stops while overlaying a solo. It made me play twice as hard and twice as good. My brother would often pick a fight with me when I was about to record a solo. I didn't find out until a long time afterward that he did it deliberately to goad me into a more emotional output.

The leadoff track on the album was a small solo guitar piece that I called "Gypsy." It was reprised at the end of the record as "Romanoff." The tune was heavily influenced by the jazz guitarists I was listening to at the time. They included Kenny Burrell, Charlie Byrd, and Gabor Szabo. I used my Flying V guitar. It was hardly a jazz guitar, but I got the correct tone by lowering the volume of my guitar to take away the power of the pickups so that I had an almost pure guitar sound.

One of the album tracks, "Sitting an' Thinking," started out with lyrics, but the vocals sounded too soft. I changed it into an instrumental, with Dave being inventive and coming up with the idea to play slide. It is a tactic I've often used up to the present time. The same thing happened with the song "Close to Midnight" on the 2017 album *Witchy Feelin'*. That morphed from a song with vocals to an instrumental for exactly the same reasons as "Sitting an' Thinking." I find that very little has changed for me through the years regarding my recording style. I use the same tactics today that I used those many years ago.

I taught myself some of the basic skills of playing piano because there was always a piano available at gigs, and it was easy to practice during the boring hours between arriving and playing a show. I decided to play piano on a song I had written named "Money Can't Save Your Soul." The lyrics to the song also had a philosophical approach that reflected my true thoughts. I've always thought that money should have a place in life, of course, but I more often see it in the biblical sense as the root of all evil.

*Looking In* seemed to be close to completion but seemed to need just one more song to make it complete. It was a Sunday, and the last planned day of the recording session was about to end. At the last minute, I threw in the idea of recording a jazzy instrumental. It worked out very well, and I called it "Sunday Night." That track, once again, gave me a chance to show off my influences, particularly Grant Green, whom I considered next in line to Wes Montgomery as a jazz guitarist. Roger Earl's jazzy drumming style was superb on "Sunday Night," and the album had its last song at the last moment.

Altogether, *Looking In* was a huge success, and it spent months on the Billboard charts and eventually broke into the Top 50 and ended up as high as #39. It was a big step forward.

During this time, I got married for the first time. Before I had left England for my first American tour, my parents had warned me about not getting caught up too early with a girl, but of course, I ignored their advice. I met Madeline at the Cafe Au Go Go in New York City. She was attracted to Dave but settled on me. I was warned that she may have been too young for me and was in it just for the fun. However, I took her back to England with me and we got married. I bought a country home in Sussex. At the time, it was very fashionable to move to the countryside surrounding the city of London. As well as being fashionable, it went along with an increase in status and earnings ratio for many musicians. I also bought a brand-new car . . . a white Mini Clubman. It was a redesigned Mini with a new front-end look and, for the first time, a Mini with windup windows set in padded doors! I loved it. It was easy to drive and park when I traveled to central London. I was being very conservative with the car. I was asked why I hadn't bought a used Mercedes for the same price.

I answered, "I wanted no fuss, no problems, easy maintenance, and a NEW car." It certainly wasn't a Bentley or a Roller. My friends thought I was being "square" and not "rock and roll" enough.

My new house was also conservative, at least compared to some of my new-money musician friends who had bought huge estates with servant quarters and guesthouses. Mine was a bungalow in style! I figured I was being somewhat frugal and that such an approach would keep me in good stead. I hoped to emerge from my success with some money left and without a huge tax bill. I kept telling Harry to let me know if I had to be worried about my future. I wanted a heads-up in case the end of my career was nigh.

I've always had the feeling that I had only two years left of my career. It was only when I got to my fifties that I started to relax by realizing I was going to be doing this for the rest of my life and not going back to a government job.

My new house was made of cedar and not the usual brick-and-mortar found in most British homes. It gave me a chance to relax. The backyard lawn was secluded, and I loved the feeling of being away from the hustle and bustle of London. However, I was still within easy driving distance of the capital. Horsham was the closest big town. I felt I had a chance of finally settling down, but that wasn't to be. Inside, I was still going 100 miles per hour while pretending that cruising at 40 was my style.

The marriage lasted a short time. It wasn't a great love. It was, in fact, just two young people having fun. I should never have gotten married. When I eventually divorced, it was a quick affair. I lost money from my bank account and money from the sale of the house. It was quite a financial and personal disaster, but I wasn't fazed by it all. I simply moved on, hand in hand with destiny, moving at such a fast pace that very few people could keep up with me.

I continued to tour the band with gigs in Europe and the USA. *Looking In* had become the band's highest-charting album to date, and I think the rock edge must have made it more appealing to mainstream audiences than the cooler and jazzier previous release of *Raw Sienna*. The album even sold reasonably well in the UK but didn't chart higher than #50. The band was still more appreciated in the United States.

As was usually the case, I immediately started writing new material following the release of *Looking In*, and I tentatively took the group into the studio to test out some of the new songs. They didn't quite fit. I was moving into a more sophisticated rhythm-and-blues direction and away from the more overt rock sounds best suited for the current band lineup. I was quite selfish in regard to playing music that I wanted to play, and I wasn't thinking of the other players in the band. Something new was growing inside me. The muse was pushing me on. I didn't quite understand what was happening, but I was driven by an inner musical desire to create something new. I needed to move on from what I and the band had already accomplished.

Unfortunately, very quickly, it became apparent that the four-piece lineup left me limited options for growth. The band could rock, but subtlety

Ewell Newton Macaulay football team, September 1959. *Back row*: Ron Trusscot, unknown, Boyce, unknown, Steven Langbridge, and unknown; *front row*: Kim Simmonds, Chris Standen, Richard Lutechford, Andrew Cran, and Bobby Walker. *Photo courtesy of Richard Lutechford; photographer unknown*

First photo of Savoy Brown Blues Band, 1965. *Left to right*: Leo Mannings, Ray Chappell, Brice Portius, John O'Leary, and Kim Simmonds. *Photo by Harry Simmonds*

First Savoy Brown record. *Photo courtesy of Mike Vernon, MBE*

Early Savoy Brown Blues Band, 1966. *Left to right*: Kim Simmonds, Ray Chappell, Leo Manning, Martin Stone, and Bryce Porteus. *Photo courtesy of Brian Wilcock; photographer unknown*

*Left to right*: Leo Mannings, Ray Chappell, Brice Portius, John O'Leary, and Kim Simmonds, 1967. *Photo courtesy of Joseph Pereira; photographer unknown*

Savoy Brown, 1968. *Left to right*: Bob Hall, Lonesome Dave Peverett, Rivers Jobe, Roger Earl, and Kim Simmonds. *Photo by Rene Legrand*

Kim Simmonds, 1970. *Photo courtesy of William Heideman*

Kim Simmonds and Dave Walker, 1971. *Photographer unknown*

Kim Simmonds and Savoy Brown, Northern Illinois University, DeKalb, Illinois, October 11, 1972.
*Photo by Jim Summaria*

Kim Simmonds and Miller Anderson, Winterland Ballroom, San Francisco, California, June 1, 1974.
*Photo by David Miller*

Savoy Brown, the Auditorium Theatre, Chicago, Illinois, April 5, 1975. *Photo by Jim Summaria*

Savoy Brown, the Auditorium Theatre, Chicago, Illinois, April 5, 1975. *Photo by Jim Summaria*

*Left to right*: Jimmie Dagnesi, Dave Walker, Alan Macomber, and Kim Simmonds, August 18, 1987, Sneakers Nightclub, San Antonio, Texas. *Photographer unknown*

*Left to right*: Jimmie Dagnesi, Dave Walker, Alan Macomber, Kim Simmonds, and Stephen Stills, August 18, 1987, Sneakers Nightclub, San Antonio, Texas. *Photographer unknown*

Kim Simmonds and Hubert Sumlin at Showplace Studios, New Jersey, 1994. *Photographer unknown*

Savoy Brown at Daryl's House, Pawling, New York, December 16, 2003. *Photo by John Shelmet*

Kim at his childhood home in Newbridge, Wales, August 23, 2003. *Photo by Andy Ford*

Kim's guitars: Bacorn Custom (hand-painted by Kim), 1991 Gibson SG, Flying V, and Gibson J-199, October 2003. *Photo by Dennis Cotton*

2004 San Francisco Blues Festival British Blues All-Stars: Gerry Sorrentino, Dave Malachowski, Rod Price, Kim Simmonds, Bob Hall, Long John Baldry, and Dennis Cotton. *Photo courtesy of Dennis Cotton*

Kim at John Shelmet's home in Pennington, New Jersey, October 7, 2005. *Photo by John Shelmet*

Boulton Center for the Performing Arts, Bayshore, New York, December 15, 2007. *Photo by Pat Martin*

Kim at a painting retreat with artist Stapleton Kearns, October 2009. *Photographer unknown*

Oops! 98 bottles of beer on the wall!

Photo by Bob Hakins 10/16/2012 @ Biscuits & Blues

Kim Simmonds of Savoy Brown

Biscuits and Blues, San Francisco, March 22, 2010. *Photo by Bob Hakins*

Kim at the Palace Theater, Syracuse, New York, April 12, 2012. *Photo by John Shelmet*

Rock 'n' Blues Fest, Beekman Beer Garden Beach Club, New York, August 8, 2012. *Photo by Arnie Goodman*

*Right*: Rock 'n' Blues Fest, Spyglass Ridge Winery, Sunbury, Pennsylvania, August 10, 2012. *Left to right*: Rick Derringer, Johnny Winter, Kim Simmonds, and Edgar Winter. *Photo by Arnie Goodman*

Windsor Blues Fest, Windsor, Ontario, Canada, July 13, 2013. *Photo by Arnie Goodman*

Genesee Theater, Waukegan, Illinois, August 10, 2014. *Photo by Jim Summaria*

SubCat Studios, Syracuse, New York, recording *The Devil to Pay* album, April 22, 2015. *Photographer unknown*

Savoy Brown, Whippany, New Jersey, December 12, 2015. *Photo by John Shelmet*

Triple Door Saloon, Seattle, Washington, March 18, 2015. *Photo by Chuck Tuck*

Iridium Jazz Club, New York, December 1, 2017. *Photo by Stefan Sousa*

Julian California Blues Festival, June 18, 2016. *Photo by Jon Naugle*

Caerphilly Castle, Wales, September 28, 2016. *Left to right*: Gerry Sorrentino, Kim Simmonds, Dave Malachowski, Dennis Cotton, and Bob Hall. *Photo courtesy of Dennis Cotton*

Garnet Grimm, Kim Simmonds, and Pat DeSalvo, the Brauer House, Lombard, Illinois, December 1, 2018. *Photo by Jim Summaria*

Kim Simmonds and Roger Earl at the Arcada Theater, St. Charles, Illinois, March 16, 2018. *Photo by Candie Kates*

Record Collector, Bordentown, New York, October 10, 2018. *Photo by John Shelmet*

Kim Simmonds and John O'Leary, Beaverwood, Chislehurst, England, January 14, 2020. *Photographer unknown*

Skyloft, Albany, New York, December 20, 2019. *Photo by John Shelmet*

Syracuse, New York, 2020. *Photo by Juan Junco*

*Melody in G Acrylic on Canvas.*
*https://www.artsy.net/artist/kim-simmonds*

*Guitar in Yellow Oil on Canvas.*
*https://www.artsy.net/artwork/kim-simmonds*

was getting lost. I was becoming an adept player with blues, rock, and jazz influences. I wanted to explore all those sides of myself and the full musical spectrum. I did not want to play in a simple rock/blues direction favored by my fellow bandmates. I wanted to explore a more rhythm-and-blues and sophisticated approach to my future musical output. It all came to a head at a Fillmore West concert. It was obvious that it was they and I, musically speaking. In a blind fit of angst, I fired everyone that afternoon at sound check.

It was a troubling time because I made the lineup change petulantly, reacting to my inner feelings, and not in an adult or thought-out manner. I simply let the musicians go, with no idea what I was going to do next. Instinctively, I knew I had to make a change. I wanted to climb another mountain. The band lineup that recorded *Looking In* lasted hardly a year. Dave, Roger, and Tony stayed together and flew home to England the next day. They asked road manager Brian to join them, but he remained faithful to me.

I had to make new plans, and I had no idea what they would be. Something was propelling me on. I certainly had great belief in myself. I was leaping ahead into the future and didn't care where I would land.

# CHAPTER 15

## A STOPGAP LINEUP, *STREET CORNER TALKING*, AND ANOTHER CLOSE SHAVE

Tell Automatic Slim, tell Razor Totin' Jim . . .

—Willie Dixon

After breaking up the band, I was back in England writing songs while Harry continued to take care of business. I was involved in putting a new band together because we had obligations to tour the USA. I'm sure Harry had finances mainly on his mind, but I was oblivious to those realities. I lived in an ivory tower.

What was I to do about a new band lineup? Harry came to my aid and first suggested that I work with Paul Raymond, the keyboardist from the band Chicken Shack. That band was going through its own changes, since its leader, guitarist Stan Webb, was also in the midst of shaking up his band's personnel. Harry managed Chicken Shack, and, following his suggestion, I got together with Paul to see if there would be any chemistry between the two of us. Paul was originally from a pop music background and had moved into the blues scene. He still had pop sensibilities, and that balanced my purist blues roots. At our first meeting, I outlined a few of the song ideas I had. One of them was the song "Tell Mama." I started to explain the idea I had for the song and picked up an unamplified guitar to play what I had so far. At that time, I'm not sure that I owned an acoustic guitar, and I did not have a piano. To write songs, I'd use what I had at hand . . . my stage guitar without an amplifier.

"I like it," Paul said. "Let's see what I can add to make it better." I had a good storyline in the lyrics and the verse and chorus. I had the feel of the tune but not much else. Paul added the details. It was a good collaboration. We were able to write well together, and that was the whole idea. "Tell Mama" became a hit for the band, later on, in 1972. I also had another excellent song with a good storyline . . . that would eventually become "Street Corner Talking."

I then enlisted Pete Scott as the new singer. He was a fine vocalist and knew quite a lot about blues music. He brought in some new ideas, and I was happy to work with him on his song ideas such as "Bluesing King" and "Blues on the Ceiling." I added Andy Pyle on bass and Ron Berg on drums, a rhythm section that had already worked as a team in the band Blodwyn Pig. I now had a new band and some new songs. Without skipping a beat, I immediately played a few gigs in England before it was time again for a long tour of the United States.

You can get to know people very well and have an impression of them. However, once you're under pressure and in a working environment, those impressions can change. As soon as I took the band to America, the leaks started to appear within the band. Personality clashes were predominant, but there was also a lack of professionalism in some cases. The tour lasted almost two months, and the Faces, with Rod Stewart and Ronnie Wood aboard, were the co-headliners, while The Grease Band opened the show. The Faces were a wonderful band.

I had a very strong musical group, but there may have been questions about the set list. I would deliberately not play songs that people wanted to hear. "Louisiana Blues" was one of those songs, and the crowd stormed close to the stage in excitement the one time I did play it. Ronnie Wood asked me why I didn't play the song every night. I didn't have an answer. I was looking to the future all the time. Playing something for obvious reasons didn't gel with my highbrow art sensibilities.

The Faces were a fun-loving and happy band. They were a great group of guys, and they were pranksters. If they decided your hotel room was going to be the after-gig party room, watch out! They would, in good nature, trash the room to leave a big mess for the unlucky occupant to explain to the front desk the next morning. Their main trick, once in the party room, was to rearrange the hotel furniture in novel and crazy ways. I kept my distance! My shyness also put some of the distance between myself and those around me. It kept me from being able to communicate with any of the other bands on tour on any meaningful level. If I did try, my awkwardness was apparent. I didn't make any friends. I did do some gigs with Ian McLagan many, many years later, when he had a solo career going. He was still great fun to be around, and I was then mature enough to have a very real connection with him the second time around.

I got through the tour, but it was obvious the band was a stopgap and didn't have any staying power. I experimented with playing shows with that band performing new songs, but I never did go into the studio to record. In the end, I caught the first plane out of New York City. It had been hard work, and I hadn't had much fun.

Paul Raymond was still a good partner, and we knew we would stay together. However, we had to find other members. With Paul as a foil for me, it then became apparent I could bring in the rest of Chicken Shack into the band.

I'd have an immediate lineup and would be able to carry on again without skipping a beat. Therefore, former Chicken Shack members Andy Silvester (bass) and Dave Bidwell (drums) became the newest members of Savoy Brown. Andy suggested I consider Dave Walker as the singer. Dave had made records with a Midlands act known as the Bow Street Runners. Andy had played a 45 rpm single featuring Dave doing a Chuck Berry song, "I'm Talking About You." Dave's voice was excellent, and I made the decision to include him as a member to round out the next version of Savoy Brown. We started rehearsing the new album material immediately.

Brian Wilcock was still my road manager and main ally. He suggested we record the Willie Dixon song "Wang Dang Doodle" for the next album. I jumped on that idea, and it became part of the rehearsal process. We also took Al Green's arrangement of "I Can't Get Next to You" as another cover song. Everyone credits me with the arrangement on that song, but that wasn't the case. Those two cover songs, added to my new compositions, made for a nicely balanced mix of songs that would eventually be released on Parrot Records (a subsidiary of Decca) in September 1971. The title of the album came from one of my songs . . . "Street Corner Talking."

I rehearsed the band every day leading up to the *Street Corner Talking* recording sessions. Rehearsals went on for weeks. Dave's voice would be hoarse after singing the songs multiple times while we got the arrangements just right. Rehearsals were a daily affair and became almost like a "nine-to-five job." There would be a stop at the local pub after a few hours of rehearsal, and we'd get back to work after a few pints of beer. We'd return to the pub at the end of the day for more pints of beer and a game or two of darts before heading home. That schedule made the process fun, and I continued that format for rehearsals through the 1970s.

The band began a highly successful and commercial period with Dave Walker singing. It didn't hurt that *Street Corner Talking* had the perfect collection of songs. It was a perfect mix of blues and rock and roll. It is difficult for me to get that blend just right, but it perfectly expresses what I feel inside when I do. In addition, that mix tends to connect with a broad audience. I feel as if I'm not being true to my roots if there is too much rock and roll, but I also feel like I'm living in the past if there is too heavy a dose of pure blues. A great mixture, when you get it right, is a beautiful thing.

We chose Olympic Studios to record *Street Corner Talking*, primarily because many successful artists had already recorded there. The Jimi Hendrix albums and the first Steve Miller Band album come to mind as products of Olympic Studios. It was good practice to use a studio that had a track record. We were thinking that some of that successful history might rub off on our project.

The album was recorded live in the studio in roughly three days. It went on to become a huge worldwide seller and still sells to this day. The incessant band rehearsals, leading to every note on every song being in place, made for a very quick and easy recording.

We recorded with engineer George Chkiantz and producer Neil Slaven. George had worked with Led Zeppelin and many classic acts. Neil had recorded my first studio session and was good for continuity. All the work had been done in the rehearsal room. Every bass note had been worked out, and all the drum patterns were firmly in place. The actual recording was a relative breeze, but there was still plenty of room for improvisation. Almost every one of my solos were first takes, including the seven-minute ballad "All I Can Do (Is Cry)."

"All I Can Do (Is Cry)" was a song I wrote about a failed relationship. She was a beautiful Danish girl named Helga. I had been involved with her for a brief period in the 1960s, and I brought her to London. We ended up getting a flat together, but I was way too domestic for her. She wanted to have fun. I met her again years later, and she said that she never thought it would work out for a long-term relationship. The lost love song prompted by that relationship was very long, with minimal verses and long extended solos. The band was rehearsed so well on the song that we decided to record it live with no overdubs whatsoever . . . and that's how it went down. I even used the reverb on the amplifier to sweeten the sound, as opposed to using the much more refined studio reverb. Engineer George wasn't happy with that, since he didn't have production control. He was stuck with whatever sound I gave him, and it all worked perfectly. I'm not sure anyone will ever reproduce a rhythm-and-blues/rock ballad with such musical content, recorded live in one take, ever again. Drummer Dave Bidwell had loose rivets put into his ride cymbal to add sizzle to the quiet sections. That is a brilliant sound, and an idea pinched from the great blues drummers prior to him. Hardly anyone does that these days. It's a subtlety lost in a modern musical world.

I used a Stratocaster guitar and a Twin Reverb amplifier for some of the *Street Corner Talking* sessions, and the album was recorded in three days. I had switched to a Stratocaster because of, you guessed it, Eric Clapton. He was still a big influence on me. He was the blues version of the Beatles to me. What he did, I did, albeit with my own personality. However, that influence was beginning to peak, since I wasn't as interested in his solo albums, although I still bought them, as much as his work in the early days with the Yardbirds, John Mayall, and Cream. I bought my Twin Reverb in the United States and brought it back to England with me. It was completely stock, and so was the Stratocaster. That is to say, my equipment was as it came from the factory. Anyway, the album and song were huge hits. I once even heard "All I Can Do" done as Muzak in an elevator!

"Tell Mama" was a radio hit. It had a Chuck Berry boogie guitar underlay. I used my Les Paul Junior for solo slide guitar playing. I used the Les Paul on the songs that needed a beefier guitar tone, and I used the Fender Stratocaster for more-subtle and cleaner tones. It was the first time I ever played slide guitar, and I found it was an approach that came very easily to me. The guitar solo arrangement on the introduction to "Tell Mama," along with the band "stops" in the background, was an idea I took from Berry's "Johnny B. Goode." Playing it as slide guitar made it sound totally different and added that touch of originality.

Paul Raymond, although primarily a keyboardist, played rhythm guitar and also soloed with me on "Tell Mama" in the middle section. He also sang harmonies on the chorus, and it was quite a talented effort. Dave's vocal pitch reached high A on the chorus, and that really set the song off. His gritty voice was perfect for the story of leaving home and going out into the world alone. I played an extended solo, but we had to abbreviate it for a single release. The song became a radio hit, but the label didn't have the clout to really push the song up the charts. We had to settle for #83 on the Billboard pop charts.

Dave didn't like and didn't want to sing "Let It Rock (Rock and Roll on the Radio)." He thought it to be a bad Elvis Presley song, but I liked it and so did Paul. The answer was for Paul to sing it. I had no confidence in my own singing at the time. It worked with Paul at the microphone and was a nice vocal change of pace for the listener. For that song, I was influenced by the Bo Diddley song "Road Runner," which had a similar bass line. In the verse, I mentioned Sticks McGhee, an artist that I liked. I've always enjoyed dropping names of musicians I like into song verses. I did it most recently on the 2017 *Witchy Feelin'* album, in which I mentioned Jimmy Reed in the song "Vintage Man."

Prior to the release of *Street Corner Talking*, I toured the band with gigs in the UK, followed by a US tour. The audience loved the new band lineup, and Dave was the perfect front man to sing and sell the music. He connected with the audience. Long John Baldry was on the bill on one tour and would watch our show from the wings. "Wang Dang Doodle" was a spectacular live song and had a chorus the whole audience could sing along with:

All night long
All night long
We're gonna pitch a wang dang doodle
All night long

I added an original arrangement at the end of "Wang Dang Doodle." We'd go into a full-tilt boogie rhythm to take the song out. Singer Dave always got the whole crowd to thrust their fists in the air as we boogied on that song. When Baldry saw the crowd raising their fists in the air, singing the chorus of the song, he quipped, "Bloody well looks like a Nuremberg rally." It *was* an amazing sight. Crowds were now getting bigger than ever. I'd never felt as good onstage with the audiences responding so loudly. Was this better than sex? Perhaps not, but it was close! I certainly was enjoying myself. I was drinking too much at times and not handling it very well. Success was certainly going to my head. There was one incident that wasn't so funny, or uplifting, and it might have spelled death or, at least, serious injury at one of these concerts. I was doing a show at the Academy of Music in New York City. The house was packed, and everyone was boogeying with the band. In the 1970s, there were almost no restrictions on what an audience member could bring to their seat . . . at least, that's how it seemed to me. Therefore, people were drinking their own wine, and the smell of marijuana was in the air. The band was coming to the very end of the show, and I was about to play the final chord to end the performance. Suddenly I caught sight of something out of the corner of my eye, and I fell back instinctively. Something hit me in the chest, just missing my vintage Stratocaster guitar and, more importantly, my face. I was in shock, and I staggered onstage, trying to stay upright. One thought immediately going through my mind was wondering if I had been shot! Then, I looked down on the floor and saw an empty Jack Daniels bottle. Someone had thrown it from the audience, and it was aimed at me! A hush descended on the crowd, from what had been a screaming madhouse a minute earlier. Walker leaped into the front seats and tried to get to the perpetrator. I imagined he must have seen the whole thing.

It was the end of the night, and we were ushered straight backstage into the dressing room. The bottle must have connected with me in a way that minimized damage to myself and my guitar. I informed everyone that I was OK. Nothing was broken, but I was very shaken emotionally that someone would throw a heavy bottle my way. My heart was sad, and I took it personally. The band and crew discussed it, and I really don't remember the course the conversations took, but we were all mad and heated up. A half hour went by, and we were all still in the dressing room and wondering about the incident. The back door leading to an outside alley was open. I was aimlessly looking that way when I saw four men walking toward the door. They approached timidly and started to apologize to me.

The man in front said, "I'm so sorry. We were having such a good time that I waved my arms around and the bottle went flying out of my grip. It headed your way and was a total accident! What can I do?"

I waved his angst away and said, "I've survived; no harm done; let's move on."

They all were grateful and relieved at my response. They had unloaded their conscience, and I had retained four fans. I was surprised, after remembering the empty bottle, that they all weren't crazy drunk. I was also relieved that there were no bad intentions behind my getting hit with a bourbon bottle. Most of all, I was happy to walk away with no harm done and to be able to tell another tale.

# CHAPTER 16

## *HELLBOUND TRAIN*, *JACK THE TOAD*, *GRACELAND*, AND A HOTEL STORY

If you want to succeed, you should strike out on new paths, rather than travel the worn paths of accepted success.

—John D. Rockefeller

The album *Hellbound Train* followed in 1972, and it became a Top 40 hit. The title track was more than nine minutes long. It was an opus. I was now moving into a more sophisticated songwriter territory and widening my approach rather than writing from a strict blues guitarist standpoint. The songs on this new album were certainly not blues songs, although many had blues as a root.

Listening to The Temptations during their psychedelic phase influenced my writing of the album's title song. They recorded a few long and socially conscious songs, and I wanted to do one of my own. The Vietnam War was going strong in 1971, and for years, soldiers had been coming to me saying how much help Savoy Brown albums had been for them to get through the hell of war. So, "Hellbound Train" reflected that kind of hell as well as being a theme I had heard in earlier blues songs such as "Hellhound on My Trail" by Robert Johnson. The song title actually came from a Robert Bloch short story. I read a lot of science fiction and horror books, and that influence can be seen on some of the Savoy Brown album covers. Those covers and the heavy song material eventually influenced the British heavy-metal bands that later appeared.

Bassist Andy Silvester helped me with the arrangement both of "Hellbound Train" the song and *Hellbound Train* the album. Andy was a very good musician and helped quite a bit with the translation of my ideas. He had well-groomed, long, brownish hair and a quiet sense of humor. He talked with a Midlands accent, which he used to exaggerate for comic effect. I suppose, to me, he was enigmatic.

I used the same Fender Stratocaster guitar on the "Hellbound Train" song that I had used on the previous record, *Street Corner Talking*, but I switched to a Les Paul Junior for the end solo. My brother thought of the idea of stopping the track abruptly at the end, to suggest that the protagonist had now gone into the blackness of hell itself. It was a remarkable idea to float and to imagine at the time. The album was recorded at Trident Studios, with Roy Thomas Baker engineering and Neil Slaven producing again. Roy had been an assistant engineer on my very first album, years previously, so there was a nice continuity there. He went on to become one of England's greatest record producers. His work with the Cars comes immediately to mind.

When it came time to mix the album, Roy suggested that the bass and drums be emphasized, a novel idea at the time. The album became Savoy Brown's highest-charting album ever. I wasn't in the mood to play a lot of guitar during this time period and was more into the role of being the songwriter. That's why there is so little guitar playing on this album. I was happy to let everyone else play. Unfortunately, in that kind of situation, you become somewhat of a bystander in your own band, and that creates its own sort of problems. I came under heavy criticism from my inside group of people for making this somewhat non-rock or non-blues album. I took that criticism to heart and didn't pursue the same course afterward.

It was difficult to play the song "Hellbound Train" live because it had a downer vibe compared to the other material the band normally played. It certainly wasn't a blues or boogie tune. *Hellbound Train*, the album, was a real turning point for me. I was going down a road that even I couldn't quite understand. The song ideas were coming to me in an organic way. To this day, I don't know how I wrote them, and I had no answer for Andy every time he asked me how I did so. He was as puzzled as I was.

It's a fact that Andy Sylvester's input to the music during this period can't be underestimated. He also worked a lot with Dave Bidwell in order to work out the right drum parts. However, despite working so well musically, Andy and I had very little personal chemistry together. He was from the

Midlands, Kidderminster, and was much closer to singer Dave Walker since they both grew up in the same part of the country. I also felt he really wanted to be a guitar player, affording him a role that would give him more spotlight. Perhaps there was resentment there, but that's only conjecture on my part. I had a deep-rooted feeling that he didn't respect me. Either way, we had no significant friendship to go along with the close music ties.

Drummer Dave Bidwell was a fantastic blues drummer. He had a great feel and touch. He wasn't a player with great technical ability, but you don't need that to make great music. He had long dark hair and sported a cool black goatee. His eyes sparkled with intelligence. They were blue and mischievous. I socialized with him and his wife, Patty, quite a bit. We often went to the best Indian restaurants together. Patty was a wild girl and counterbalanced Dave's laid-back personality. Patty was definitely a Marilyn Monroe type. It makes me wonder why the drummers in the band invariably were my friends. I've always liked drummers and have an affinity with them that I can't really explain.

Drummer Dave's past did include problems with drugs, but they seemed to have cleared up by this time. He was earning good money, had gotten married, and was driving a nice Mercedes. I often shared a room with him on the road. He did have unusual sleeping habits. In fact, I'm not sure he slept at all! He once told me he had stayed up for days and days without sleeping. Often I'd wake up to use the bathroom in the middle of the night and I'd see Dave, wide awake, polishing his shoes. Perhaps he was using drugs, but I didn't know. That lifestyle was alien to me. Dave had a drug conviction from earlier days that I found out about only when it got in the way of us touring in Australia. Other than that, it didn't seem to interfere, and the band rolled on.

Paul Raymond had started his career with the pop band Plastic Penny and had then joined Chicken Shack during the British blues boom period. Paul was of medium height with medium-long hair and had an acute sense of style. His face was round, and he had dark eyes. He always dressed smartly, preferring flamboyant coats that he wore onstage and for street wear. We became friends. It helped that he lived, with his wife, Maggie, close to me. We were able to socialize as well as be bandmates. He stayed with me through the whole of the 1970s. Musically, he did everything well. His songwriting was also very strong. His playing dominated on the *Hellbound Train* songs as I became less interested in being a guitar hero.

Singer Dave Walker was a likable man with a fine sense of humor. He seemed permanently dissatisfied with life, and that fueled his humorous side. His brown hair was long and flowing, and he liked to tuck his jeans into long boots. He was definitely a jeans-and-denim-shirt guy. In fact, he was to later write a song on the *Lion's Share* album called "Denim Demon." His tough, no-holds-barred personality made him the best performance front man I've ever had in the band. He also added strength and manliness to my compositions. I was lucky to have him singing the songs.

The *Hellbound Train* album sold well . . . the best to date. In fact, the title song stands up today. Recently, at a gig, a young guy, seeing the band for the first time, was thrilled after hearing the tune for the first time. He asked what song the band had just played. I told him, and he immediately bought the CD that included a live version. If you listen to songs such as "Stranglehold" by Ted Nugent, and other songs like that, you'll hear (I think) the influence of the song "Hellbound Train." Disney almost bought the song from me for a big movie they were doing. It didn't materialize, but I imagine, one day, a producer will discover the song, and we'll all hear it in the mainstream once again.

Despite the success of *Hellbound Train*, my brother and producer Neil Slaven thought I had better get back to familiar blues roots for my next album. I couldn't see, from an objective standpoint, where I had settled from an artistic standpoint. Therefore, I took their advice and started writing more songs with a harder blues edge and less of a lighter and poppy approach. The change stopped my progression as a "progressive" writer, and I don't think I ever quite regained that ability until years later. Harry later agreed that it had been a mistake to advise me to change direction back to a more overt blues-writing style.

While everything around *Hellbound Train* and its aftermath was happening, we were playing gigs. As time moved on into the 1970s, I took the band into Carnegie Hall, to concerts in Central Park, and into dozens of classic theaters around the country, playing to thousands of people. The show was always focused on the band and the songs I had going at that time. I'd play no songs from the past.

My life was somewhat steady, and, heeding advice, I went into the studio and recorded the *Lion's Share* album with its more traditional blues song base. The record was a return to familiar ground. I came up with the title, hoping it would suggest much to the imagination. It was my second album in the year 1972, and I simply hadn't enough time to digest where I was or where I was heading. I wasn't in a "song muse" headspace and didn't have many ideas. An outside song, "Shot in the Head," was suggested to me, and I accepted it. It had been written by the Australian songwriting duo of Vanda and Young. Harry Vanda and George Young were members of the 1960s Australian rock group The Easybeats. George was the older brother of AC/DC's guitarist, Angus Young. It seemed I had a connection with the band, albeit from a distance. I played slide guitar on "Shot in the Head," and it was similar to "Tell Mama" in that it had a boogie guitar base, slide guitar, and a strong verse and chorus structure. *Lion's Share* was rounded out with two covers of classic blues tunes, a couple of Paul Raymond songs, and a few of my own compositions.

I was now married for the second time and actually wrote a song on this album about that. I called it "Second Try." Another song I wrote was titled "So Tired," and the lyrics summed up the fact that I was feeling totally burned out after a decade of intense music making. My favorite composition on *Lion's Share* is the blues ballad "Love Me Please."

The album, because it followed two previous commercial offerings, was never going to compete on that level, and it wasn't meant to. *Lion's Share* was an attempt to recapture the old muse, although I fear that muse had left me temporarily. Therefore, the release never had the total artistic complexity of earlier albums. I promoted the album, but it fared poorly on the charts, and it coincided with further band members leaving or being fired . . . a familiar refrain by now.

Andy Silvester finally got on the wrong side of me, and I let him go. We were rehearsing for a follow-up album to *Hellbound Train*. He was now suggesting material such as "You Can't Sit Down" by Phil Upchurch and others. I felt he was looking for more control within the group and was not supporting me in the way I needed. It led to a confrontation, and I realized he no longer acknowledged me as the leader of the band. I responded as the boss, and he was fired. Dave Walker then left the band. Rumors were circulating that I might be changing singers, and he made a preemptive strike and left before any changes came. Would I have let Dave go? He was acting differently now that he had achieved some success, and he had become uncommunicative. I'm sure I complained to others, and, perhaps, word got around. The other factor involved was Fleetwood Mac. We had toured a lot with the band, and Dave became close to the members. They lured Dave away and he joined the band, but it didn't work out. I don't think they were prepared to give Dave the reins, so to speak. They wanted to use him in a limited capacity, and they already had huge talent in the band. In Savoy Brown, Dave had been given plenty of creative space to sing, perform, and lead the band from the stage each night.

Nevertheless, I was now enjoying life around me. Harry kept me in the dark regarding the finances, but the extra money I was earning was good. I bought a new house and a new car. I was oblivious to the business going on behind me. I was a rock-and-roll star.

Now that singer Dave had joined Fleetwood Mac, what was going to be my next move? Brian came to my aid and suggested the singer Jackie Lynton as a replacement. I remembered Jackie from records he had made in the early 1960s . . . before the Beatles. I figured he was an old-school rocker. One rainy night, Brian took me to a local club, and I heard Jackie sing with his band. He did some original songs that I really liked, and I thought they would be great to record with Savoy Brown. I offered Jackie the job, he accepted, and we started rehearsing. His songs sounded wonderful, and there was a real influx of new energy into the band.

Jackie was quite a bit older than everyone else in the band . . . seven years older. His hair was thinning, and he'd comb it over in front to cover the fact. His sense of humor was stunning, and he was continuously funny. He could simply point out the absurdity of life around us and make us laugh uncontrollably. He had a beefy body shape and a strong London, almost Cockney, accent. At the time, he was a house painter and actually had been on the job painting John Lennon's home. He hadn't made a good living from singing, but he now had a chance to put his career on track by singing with Savoy Brown.

Paul Raymond stayed on playing keyboards, and Dave Bidwell continued on as my drummer. Andy Pyle, on bass guitar, completed the lineup. I took the band into Morgan Studios in London to record the next album, which would be titled after one of Lynton's songs, "Jack the Toad." During the recording, Dave Bidwell was replaced by drummer Ron Berg (this would be Ron's second stint with me). The change was prompted by Dave's development of erratic behavior, with, unfortunately, drug use suspected as the cause. Barry Murray, my brother Harry's partner, produced the recording. He basically let everyone get on with the music and was there more in an executive capacity . . . or so it seemed to me. I'd look into the control room, and he'd be reading the daily newspaper. I wasn't at the height of my guitar powers and didn't have the personnel around me who had the blues background that I did. It was a rock-and-roll band. I was surrounded by a group of good musicians, but there was a lack of simpatico.

I sang the song "Ride On Babe" on the album, and it was my first attempt at singing. It was a good vocal, and producer Barry likened it to a John Lee Hooker performance. I never did take the song to the stage until decades later. *Jack the Toad* fared well on the Billboard charts and was helped by quite a few television appearances to promote the album. The band appeared on the *Midnight Special* show and *Don Kirshner's Rock Concert.* I was immediately recognized by the public on the street. It's amazing what television exposure can do for your career. The live stage show at this time was very good. Again, I had the band play only the new songs that featured Jackie. I gave him the attention I thought he and the band needed to be successful.

Jackie collected keys from all the hotels we stayed at and wore them as a necklace. He was quite the character onstage, and the crowds enjoyed him, although older fans took awhile to adjust to the new singer. One day, while doing a show in Memphis, Tennessee, Jackie and I decided to go to Graceland and visit, or at least to see, the home of Elvis Presley. Jackie was a huge fan of Presley's, and I wasn't far behind. We made it over to Highway 51 South, now Elvis Presley Boulevard, and parked our car nearby. No one was around, and we walked up to the small front gates. A man was standing there, and we got into a conversation. He was a member of the Presley family and seemed to be employed as a front-gate guard. The conversation was easygoing, and Jackie got us all laughing with his great Cockney humor. The guard asked us where we were from. We were asked, "Where are you guys from?"

"We're from England," I replied. "We've come all the way to meet Elvis." He laughed. "Elvis is on tour, but why don't I show you guys around?"

I looked at Jackie, and he looked at me with a "Let's go" smile on his broad face.

"That would be great. Thank you."

I was thrilled. We were taken on a personal tour around the grounds but were told going inside was off-limits since family members were living there. It was surreal. Afterward, we gave our thanks, shook hands, and left in the best mood you can imagine. Maybe three years later, Elvis was dead. When I returned sometime after that, the crowds were huge and a police detachment guarded the front gates, which had grown to be 6 feet high. Now it is a tourist destination and has a theme park atmosphere, and you take an organized tour.

Talking of a tour, with Jackie in the band, I toured the band constantly. Commercial success was at hand. It was one hotel after another hotel, with barely a moment to shower. Hotel proprietors will tell you they see more than you can imagine dealing with guests. I, too, have had my share of unusual happenings staying in hotels, motels, guesthouses, hostels, inns, and band rooms over my long career. By the way, did I leave anything out? I've been bitten by bedbugs in fancy places. One particular memory does stand out. I was again traveling, this time in Canada. I had played a show with the band, and we had a couple of days off. It was time to slow down, relax, and enjoy some downtime. We had booked about seven or eight rooms in a row on the ground floor of a nice hotel in a downtown area. The hotel was close to restaurants and shops, and there was easy parking. It was a safe area too. These are all the things you look into before you book a hotel on the road. Theft is the number one headache when touring. You don't want to be close to the bad side of town, although the bad people will find you anyway, believe me. You also want plenty of facilities, so you don't get bored. A park is a bonus to exercise and get fresh air.

There we were, in our rooms, five band members and crew. After breakfast, the first day, we socialized by visiting each other's rooms. The hotel wasn't full, and it seemed we were the only guests on our floor. It was midweek. We could, therefore, be lackadaisical. We left our doors open (they didn't close automatically) as we all intermingled. I went over to the drummer's room and discussed song tempos and new songs I wanted to try, making sure he had the right tempos in his metronome. I was in a good mood, and after that talk, I returned to my room. I closed the door behind me and figured I'd take a nap. I washed my hands, and as I did so, I thought that something felt odd to me. It was a metaphysical feeling. A few minutes later, I still had the same feeling as I walked to the window to close the curtains. At that point, something caused me to look over my shoulder. I jumped back as I looked at the skirting around my bed. A leg was sticking out from beneath the bedsprings! I was freaked out. I ran from my room, telling my band and crewmates, "There's a dead body in my room!" You can imagine the incredulous stares that came my way. I didn't want to go back into my room alone, so I gathered a couple of helping hands. We gingerly approached the bed where the body lay. Sure enough, I hadn't imagined anything. There was the leg still in the same position. I moved closer, still not believing my eyes. I pulled back the lower covering and peered beneath the bed. There, I could see a woman. She was in a huddled position on her side, with her hands to her face. I looked closer. She was holding some kind of jar close to her nose, and the one word I could make out on the container label was large and unmistakable . . . GLUE.

I called the hotel manager. He, in turn, called the police, and a squad car arrived in a very short time. They apprised the situation immediately and confirmed that the woman in question was sniffing glue from a can. Apparently the problem had become epidemic in the area. They called the paramedics, and they, too, arrived quickly. They managed to get the woman out from under the bed, and they strapped her to a gurney. On closer inspection, as they rolled her away, I realized she was younger than I first thought, but her face was very haggard. Apparently the glue fumes had aged her tremendously. I was surprised at how professional and nonplussed the police and emergency teams had been. They told me they had seen plenty of drug incidents in their careers. It became clear from talking to them that the woman had simply walked into the hotel and down our hallway, found my door open, and, in an altered state of mind, looked for a hole to hide in. That hole turned out to be the darkness under my bed. These days, my hotel room door stays closed. I don't want to find any more surprises waiting for me lurking under where I sleep.

The band with Jackie did have its own problems. There was some unrest among the band members, and a lot of backstabbing was going on. After making one album and promoting it with many shows, the lineup started to fall apart, and yet again I was starting over. It had been coming on and was not a big surprise. I was a bandleader, and I'd seen it before. I suppose you could liken it to the 1940s big-band era, but this was the 1970s. I did what I always did . . . I moved on.

# CHAPTER 17

## BOOGIE BROTHERS, END OF A DECADE, AND IMMIGRATION

To everything, there is a season.
—Ecclesiastes 3:1–8

As the 1970s moved forward into the middle of that decade, I found myself running out of artistic steam. I had been playing nonstop while forming and re-forming the band. I wasn't practicing as I should have been. I didn't think I needed to. It's true that you never forget how to play guitar. You can put it down for a month or two, pick it up, and carry on from where you left off. That's true to an extent, but to really be on top of the instrument, you have to practice every day, no matter how good you are. Practice, practice, practice. That's how you get success, and that's how you keep it.

Recognizing that I needed help with the band, and as a musician, Harry floated an idea. I could see in his eyes that he was excited about what he was about to say. Harry invariably had a whiskey in one hand and a cigarette in the other. This day was no different. He chain-smoked and drank alcohol like nobody's business. He took a huge drag of smoke from his cigarette, mouth wide open, and swished it down with a gulp of scotch on the rocks. It was still only about 11:00 in the morning.

"I'll put you together with Stan Webb and Miller Anderson. Let's bring them into Savoy Brown, and we'll call the next album *Boogie Brothers*. The three of you will be the Boogie Brothers. What do you think? Brilliant, right?"

Both Stan and Miller were managed by Harry. Stan was the leader of Chicken Shack but wasn't doing so well at the time. Miller's solo career had also stalled a bit at the same time I was limping along artistically.

"I could see that working," I replied immediately. "Let's try it," I said enthusiastically.

It seemed to be an easy solution to my problems of being bone dry of song ideas and burned out from too much bandleading. This way, I could let Stan and Miller shoulder a lot of the responsibility. They were also bandleaders, and Miller was a good songwriter. The band was rounded out with Jimmy Leverton on bass and Eric Dillon on drums. To be honest, earlier that year, I was thinking of giving up on Savoy Brown. However, this idea made me begin to think it would be the next highlight of my career. The project started with Miller coming to my house for a jam to see if we had chemistry and could work together. We did.

Miller was Scottish and had a lovely lilting accent. He was a pleasant man with a slightly unkempt look that was attractive. His hair had that disheveled look, which he wore well. He had come to national attention as a singer and guitarist with the Keef Hartley Band. I liked him and felt comfortable moving forward with him as one of the main components.

The album *Boogie Brothers* was recorded at Island Records' Basing Street Studios in London, and I thought it was going to be a hit. Following the preliminary meetings with Miller, we very quickly went into the studio. Miller had written some excellent songs for the project. I contributed two of my own compositions, and Stan provided a classic slow blues. The sessions were a lot of fun.

At one point, Paul Kossoff, the great guitarist from the defunct band Free, showed up and wanted to participate. I sat down with him, and he was desperate to play, but it was obvious to me that his drug problems were immense. He was discombobulated and wasn't in a focused mindset. His clothes seemed to suggest he was homeless. He looked so unkempt. Reluctantly, I had to fend off his requests and tell him it wasn't possible for him to join in. I felt bad, but he was in no condition to be able to play at the high level required to be in Savoy Brown. He left dejectedly. A couple of years later, his drug problems got the best of him, and he was dead at the age of twenty-five.

The *Boogie Brothers* recording sessions went very smoothly. Everyone worked together as a team. We all were experienced, and egos were left to the side. Presumably inspired by Stan's drinking prowess and his wonderful humor when intoxicated, Miller wrote the song "Everybody Loves a Drinking Man." He also wrote a song about us all, the "Boogie Brothers." Unfortunately, almost fifty years later, I'm now completely blank regarding any actual details of the day-to-day recording sessions for *Boogie Brothers*.

As usual, there was a tour to promote and sell the record after the album was recorded. I needed to keep the band moving forward. The band Deep Purple was the king of rock and roll in 1974, and Savoy Brown was signed on to be special guests on their North American tour . . . a huge opportunity to continue at the highest level. Deep Purple rented their own jet plane to travel in. It was a Boeing 707 and was known as the Starship because so many star groups had used it to tour, including Frank Sinatra, Led Zeppelin, and Elton John, among others. The band's name was in large letters on the side of the jet. It had a lounge, a bedroom, a shower, and a room to read and relax in. I was excited. We all were due to fly on the plane together. No more domestic flights! However, at the last minute, for reasons I'm still not sure of, we were not going to fly on the Starship.

The cost of renting the plane was phenomenal, and I asked one of the Deep Purple band members why they were going to such expense. "People will recognize us and bother us in airports" was the response. I really thought that was exaggerating their appeal a little, but it was their money to waste.

The tour was great fun. Deep Purple was a top band, but they were very loud for my taste . . . you could hear them a mile away. Nevertheless, it was a pleasure to listen to such good musicians and musicians I had followed for years when they were in their start-up bands. My own band held its own, and Stan Webb would often walk into the crowd, playing guitar. That was a crowd-pleaser. I was in good form. We had good songs, and Miller Anderson could sing with the best of them. I partied a bit with some of the Deep Purple band members. It was my first introduction to cocaine. For me, it was a fun social drug, akin to drinking, and I never developed a destructive habit with the white powder. Now, drinking, that was another thing altogether. That would turn out to be my Achilles' heel.

The Deep Purple tour ended, and we continued the very next day with our own US tour, headlining over Manfred Mann's Earth Band and newcomers KISS. Manfred Mann had been around since the early 1960s and had many pop hits. By the time this tour took place, they were a serious and almost progressive rock band. KISS, of course, would go on to change the very nature of rock and roll as their career moved on through the 1970s and all the way into the new millennium. This was their first national tour. They were third on the bill. One would have thought that the Savoy Brown and Manfred Mann audience would have turned their backs on a band that painted their faces and breathed fire, but times were changing, and everyone loved them, myself included.

The tour continued along, and one night Stan was intoxicated . . . or was he just tired? Either way, he sat cross-legged on the stage. I was playing stage left and happened to look over. I couldn't see Stan, and I panicked for a few seconds. Then I spotted him sitting on the floor. He played the whole show sitting down! The tour eventually ended in early June with three dates in Alaska. It was the time of year when it never got dark in that part of the world. I went to the bar with Stan in the afternoon on the first gig, and because it was light outside, I lost my time perspective. Stan kept plying me with drinks, and by showtime I could hardly stand, let alone play. I was propped up onstage, and as I started to veer and fall into the wings, the opening act, KISS, would push me back onstage. They thought it funny, but I was embarrassed for a long time after that little fiasco.

Savoy Brown, with Stan and Miller, lasted a year, and that was amazing considering there was such an array of individual talent. After the long US tour, we returned to the UK, took a month off, and continued the tour in our home country. Eventually, there were grumblings and complaints in the dressing room. The experiment, as talented as it was, came to an end. It was all good for a season. Stan and Miller went their own ways again.

I took six months off and then decided I still wanted to play guitar. I reunited with Paul Raymond and Dave Bidwell and brought in Andy Rae on bass and vocals. Sadly, shortly thereafter, Dave passed away, and his drug-related death was a terrible tragedy. I went to his funeral, and no one else but his mother attended. It was a sad end to one of Britain's finest-ever blues drummers. Tommy Farnell replaced Dave on drums, and the juggernaut rolled on.

I was now, for the first time, fed up with getting lead singers for the band. I made the decision that Paul and I would take over those duties for the next studio release, *Wire Fire*. The standout song was "Hero to Zero," co-written by Paul and me. The sentiment is exactly how I felt at the time.

I was feeling the effects of touring, bandleading, songwriting, producing, you name it. I was just plain tired.

*Wire Fire* fared reasonably well and reached #150 on the Billboard charts. I did the usual US tour after its release. That tour included a Bottom Line club date in New York City that was recorded and released as a live album. Various acts opened the shows, including Eddie Money and Loggins and Messina. We opened for Black Sabbath for one of the shows. I did enjoy the tour. I was enjoying the life I had created. The band was excellent, and I was still playing the guitar well. That rarely failed me. The decade continued as such, with my personal life taking up much of my time. My second marriage was working, and I had two children to keep me occupied.

As the 1970s ended, Paul Raymond left the band to join UFO, and I decided not to replace him. I would continue as a three-piece outfit. Without Paul to help with vocals, I decided a lead singer would be needed again. That would turn out to be Ian Ellis, and Ian handled the vocals on *Savage Return*, the last album of the 1970s for me.

Ian was a wiry Scotsman with a wicked grin. I had known him from earlier days, when he had come down from Scotland with his first band, the Clouds. I spent time with him working up material for *Savage Return* in a house I bought in Wallingford, Surrey. For dress rehearsals, a club was rented, and one afternoon, who should show up but Chris Youlden. A fan, Frank Reda, had brought Chris along. Youlden looked enthusiastic, and Frank was full of energy. It occurred to me that this was an overture for Chris to rejoin the band. I was put in a spot. Singer Ian Ellis was looking over my shoulder. Chris was in front of me. I simply exchanged pleasantries, and the whole conversation sputtered and led nowhere. If indeed Chris was looking for conciliation, I wish he simply would have called me on the telephone or had arranged a meeting. As it was, he and fan Frank must have made a rash decision to simply show up and surprise me. Who knows what would have happened if the whole situation had been handled in a more organized fashion? I made no changes.

It was now 1979, and punk rock was taking England by storm. I was beginning to feel out of touch with my own country and the music scene. Harry tried to help the situation and pulled off another brilliant managerial move by bringing in Mutt Lange as the producer for *Savage Return*.

Mutt was already in demand and had produced many punk and new-wave bands but wanted to advance his recognition in the US market. He gave up his vacation time to produce the record. I played him some demos, and a date was set to record. The band consisted of Ian Ellis, Tommy Farnell, and myself. The recording process was the best part. Mutt chose Rockfield Studios in Monmouthshire, Wales, just bordering my home county. We rehearsed down the road from the studios in a country home that was studio owned. That was the best part. Looking back, the songs I provided had none of the blues and boogie so important to my music. Mutt had genius potential and worked the band hard to get as much as possible from the players. The songs weren't that good, and Mutt did what he could to make them more than what they were. I could tell he had great respect for my playing. I wish I could have given him more. However, I was a shell of my previous self. The spark was starting to go out. I had forgotten who I was. I had forgotten the music I should be playing. I was caught up in the music trends around me and couldn't see how I fit in. I felt like a dinosaur. I could play a twenty-minute guitar solo effortlessly, without repeating a single lick, but no one wanted that in England. That was passé. I was passé. I was gasping for air, artistically, as the decade ended.

An American tour ensued, and I don't remember much about it. I felt finished as an artist. I had to make some changes. I was married to an American girl. I felt my future was in America. There was no real work for me in Europe. The music world had moved on. For me, living in England didn't make much sense any longer. My following was in the States. I felt like I was understood in the States. I was washed up in my own country . . . passed by. I decided to immigrate to the USA. I'd go to Ohio, where my wife was from. Those around me said I was mad, and I would be killing my career.

In the UK, I was doing gigs, and the audience was literally spitting at me. New bands were coming out that couldn't play their instruments but could make an anarchist statement. It was disturbing to me, and I decided I'd had enough. Britain was less and less the country I had grown up in. The music scene bore no resemblance to what I knew, and I found myself sitting around doing nothing . . . resting on my laurels. Relations with my brother had broken down. Whenever I quizzed him on the financial end of our partnership, rows would ensue. He wasn't about to reveal, or even explain, the financial goings-on behind the scenes. I was too weak to fight him, and the thought of starting a family war wasn't an option for me. Emigrating, perhaps it could be called running away, seemed the safer conclusion to what was a very deep problem. My future was in the USA. I could remake myself and start anew. My career was in tatters, and I was low on money. I had the band name and reputation, so I made steps to move ahead. It was going to prove to be very rough sailing ahead. The waters would be cold. I'd find myself marooned, and I'd be the captain of a very waterlogged ship. I moved, household goods and all, to America.

# CHAPTER 18

## OHIO, CHALLENGES, AND I KEEP THE BAND GOING

I shall create a new world for myself.
—Frederic Chopin

The 1980s began, and I found myself living in central Ohio. I had moved my belongings, including a grand piano, via shipping containers to a brick ranch house in the middle of nowhere. It was a test for me. Here I was, previously a cosmopolitan guy living in a big city, suddenly living in the Amish country. It was an odd feeling to see my typical British home belongings, including classic leather furniture, in a typical American house. Truth was, I was lost, but it challenged me intellectually and, somewhat to my surprise, spiritually. I was always looking for help with the latter.

"You have too big a conscience," Harry once said to me. I don't know if that was a condemnation of me or a reflection of his own scant conscience. It never occurred to me how hard it would be to adjust to American living. After all, I had toured the country for years. The fast pace, let's do it NOW, and the language difference (yes, that was a surprise to me) confused me. You say "tomato" and I say "tomahto" and so on.

My professional life was put on hold, since I was more involved with my family and the new life in the USA. My guitar playing started to suffer, since I stopped practicing altogether. Had I forgotten who I was? Away from my natural environment, I was lost. I needed help. I discovered my

Christian roots and rejoined the church. I actually got baptized, since that did not occur after I was born because my parents had been agnostics. The church helped me enormously, and I was able to cling to the man inside through what was going to be a trying number of coming years.

I was living in a nice bungalow-style house in a small town. I had two young children going to school. It was a nice life, but far removed from what I was used to. I wasn't working, and I would find myself staring out the window into the fields around me. Perhaps I was looking for something I had lost. The winters were harsh, and the summers were really hot. I was surrounded by cornfields. You can't say I've been afraid of a challenge.

I adapted to the new lifestyle, and I bought my first gun. It was an all-silver handgun and a domestic version of what the police were using. I couldn't believe how available guns seemed to be and how easy it was to buy one. A friend of a friend sold it to me. I bought the gun mostly because of the novelty value. Groundhogs were a menace to farmers in my area. A local boy had recently died when his tractor had fallen through a groundhog hole. I decided I would help the local farmers and thin out the groundhog problem. The first time I used my handgun to fire at a varmint, the recoil knocked me flat on my backside. I was no Wyatt Earp. I never fired a gun again. I also had a shotgun and a rifle. It seemed fun owning something as exotic as firearms. One day, I was showing a friend my handgun, and we fooled around with it. "It's empty," I said before I checked. All the time we had been fooling around, there had been one bullet in the chamber. I sold the guns.

I was staring out of the window and isolated in my own thoughts. I was thousands of miles away from my original home. But where was that home? Wales? Sussex? London? I felt like a nomad with no real root base. The Amish community was heavily invested in the area I lived in. I found the lifestyle fascinating and would go to the farmhouses for fresh eggs and get a peep at how the families lived. Everything was done by hand. No automation. Conversation was minimal. I was part of a different world but occasionally starting to feel as if I didn't belong in any part of the world.

One summer's day, I was home in the afternoon when the phone rang. It was someone I knew who lived a few miles away.

"There's someone asking for you. He looks a bit shady."

"Should I be worried?" I asked.

"I don't know. He says he's a fan."

I wondered who the heck it could be. I paced the floor nervously. I had a feeling it was nothing to worry about. I had met my fair share of crazies in the music business. More and more phone calls came in as my neighbors were warning me that someone was looking for me and that someone was getting closer. I told them not to worry.

Eventually, a guy with long and unkempt hair showed up at my door. He wore a heavy leather jacket. His black hair was tousled, and his eyebrows were large and black and badly in need of a trim. He spoke with a Brooklyn accent. He introduced himself. His name was Frank Reda! The same person who had brought Chris Youlden to my dress rehearsal a year before. Here he was again, a huge fan of mine who had come all the way from New York City by way of a mixture of train, bus, and hitchhiking. I accepted him into my house. He obviously knew his music, and I understood straight away that he was harmless.

However, he was obsessed. We spoke for quite a while, and then he left. I have no idea how he got back home, presumably the same way he had found me. Every time I played New York City from that day on, that hitchhiking fan, Frank, was always sitting and watching from the front row.

At first, I thought it would be business as usual between Harry and me. He would simply manage me from a distance, and we'd continue. Other real-world factors were working inside me, and I hadn't brought those to the front of my mind. The relationship did continue of sorts for the first few months I was in America. Harry would send me money, and I was thinking we'd get some inspiration together to figure out the future. That never happened. The money and communication eventually dried up.

We kept in touch, but we were now in different worlds. We had always been as such, and I just didn't know it. It was the end of a relationship that, however dysfunctional, had prospered and enriched the music world. I eventually heard that Harry had gone broke and ended up in prison for a drug-trafficking offense. I sent him a package of Savoy Brown albums so he could use them as collateral in prison. My mother became ill with cancer, and I returned to Wales for a few weeks to comfort her. Harry was transferred from a high-security prison in London to a much more friendly prison in Cardiff, so as to be close to her at this time of distress.

On a rare trip back to Wales, I visited Harry in prison, and he looked fit as a fiddle. I smuggled some cigarettes in for him under the table. “Thank you, boyo,” he said, his Welsh accent still there. “Everyone does it. No problem as long as you don’t get caught.”

My mother was not in a good place. Cancer surgery had left her with a colostomy bag that never seemed to fit correctly. I made her tea every night and listened while she talked of my dad, the love of her life.

“Why didn’t he change?” she would ask me pleadingly.

“He couldn’t, mum,” I replied, taking her side. “You did your best.” My parents now lived apart on the same street of row houses in Tredegar, Wales, where they had retired to. My mom was in number 2 and my dad lived in number 21. For years, they had a routine whereby they would have breakfast, lunch, and dinner together but, otherwise, live in their own houses. My mom died shortly afterward. My dad sold his house and moved into my mom’s vacant home.

Back in Ohio, I was on my own and decided I needed to keep things going. I enlisted some local musicians to make a band lineup. It started as a fun thing to do, and we’d play a little in my basement, and I was enjoying that. It led to a realization that this could be my next band outing. Some regional agents provided gigs, and before I knew it, I was on the road playing again with musicians from Mansfield, Ohio, and the Cleveland area.

I had a road manager and a driver when touring, but I usually had to pick up the slack. One night, I took over driving because everyone was dog-tired. We had finished playing a gig and were driving overnight to the next appointment. It was about three in the morning. I was at the wheel, and it must have been 1981, because I remember Journey playing on the radio . . . one of their huge hits from that time period. The song got into my head. The lyrics were something about “believing.” The next minute I woke up, and the large conversion van was bouncing around like a crazy rollercoaster. I had fallen asleep and found myself in a deep median. Luckily for me, and for all of us, the median was deep and curved. It was deep and curved to stop wayward vehicles like my own from crossing into traffic in the opposite lanes. The design worked like clockwork. With just a little control from me, the van took the curved design, and within seconds I had driven out of the divide and was back on the highway, heading to our destination! It happened so fast that I was able to say,

"Nothing," when some bleary-eyed musicians asked what was going on. Everyone went back to sleep. Some didn't even wake up. I drove on, my heart thumping like an engine on full throttle.

There were other complications as I tried to keep the ship afloat in those days. Such was the case during a particularly trying Canadian trip I had planned one summer. Everything had been organized well ahead of time, with close attention paid to all the nuts and bolts that go into making a tour work. A good road crew had been assembled, including a sound engineer and a lighting director. The truck for the equipment and transport for the band had been ordered well in advance. The advance deposits for the upcoming shows had been received . . . half the contract money is always sent by the promoter before doing a gig or gigs.

All seemed well as I drove to meet everyone at the rehearsal room in Cleveland before we were going to leave. Some work had to be done on song arrangements and so forth, along with finalizing departure times. Such was the order of the day. These thoughts and details were going through my mind as I pulled my Volvo into the parking lot. We were actually rehearsing in a local studio owned by Kirk Yano, a friend of mine. Kirk welcomed me, and I noted that everyone else was there, band members and crew, except for the bass player. I assumed he was late, as usual. We brewed coffee and relaxed, talking about sports and the latest news, while waiting for the one errant person. We sat in the studio's green room. An hour passed . . . no bass player. A call was made to his house, and there was no answer. More coffee was poured, and I was becoming concerned. I should have been worried simply about his safety and so forth, but a negative red flag was waving in the back of my head. Another twenty minutes went by, and the wall clock chimed that another hour had passed. I started feeling anxious, and I knew that something strange was in the air. Had he been involved in an emergency, or was he simply not going to show? I wouldn't allow myself to think the worst. However, he had been acting oddly of late. I didn't think he would let me, or the band, down the day before a tour, but those negative thoughts rested in my mind. After more time passed, panic started to prevail. Everyone wondered where he could be, but they were asking me as if I had a crystal ball. However, I was the bandleader, and I had to provide leadership if not an answer.

When the church bells across the street chimed five o'clock, I knew something had to be done. Sitting around wringing our hands wasn't accomplishing anything. I sent one of the road crew to the bass player's house to see if some information could be obtained there. He did have a live-in girlfriend, and she might be helpful. The roadie returned sometime later, after going across town and back, to report there was no one at the house and all the lights were off. He left a written message in the doorjamb. I called the police station, but nothing had been reported there. I then got the idea to call the local music store where the bassist was known to frequent and was friendly with the salespeople.

"Have you seen Michael?" I asked.

"No" was the reply. "He should be in Detroit. He got an offer from Ted Nugent and decided to take it. Didn't he tell you?"

I suddenly had my answer. It was the answer I didn't want to believe, but the picture had been forming in my head. The conclusion would be hard to accept. My bass player had left me for another band and didn't have the nerve to tell me. I remembered that Ted Nugent had been at a recent show of mine, and I had seen him in earnest conversation with my bassist. It made me suspicious at the time, and now I knew I had good reason to be suspicious. Clearly, an act of piracy had now taken place. The plot was exposed, and I had to act fast. I immediately called around town to my network of musician friends, asking if they knew of a bass player who would be available for the next morning! All I got in response was a good laugh from most of them, but I got lucky on my final call. I had reached a friend in the midst of his birthday party, and he said there was a guitar player there who might be interested. I spoke to the musician, who seemed to be ready to go, so I told him to come to the studio and we'd talk.

Equipment was already set up, and before long the musician arrived. Let's call him Jim. Unfortunately, Jim had arrived drunk as a skunk! He was unable to play a note in the condition he was in, but he had come very highly recommended. The party, I guess, had gotten the better of him. I had to make a decision. I informed Jim that he was the bass player for this tour, and that he should be fully packed and ready to go by 8:00 the next morning. Everyone looked at me as if I was crazy, but they also knew the show had to go on.

The next morning, we picked up Jim. He had to be dragged out of bed. He was hardly awake, still somewhat drunk, and hardly intelligible when he tried to talk. We grabbed his bag, threw him in the back seat of the bus, and drove away fast, before he had time to reconsider. He instantly fell fast asleep and didn't wake up for many hours. When he did wake up and looked out the window, we were driving on a desolate highway somewhere in the Midwest.

Jim remembered everything vaguely—the telephone call and the rehearsal room—but couldn't quite believe where he was or where he was going. I recall him saying that it was lucky we got him when he was drunk. The rest of the day, we played tapes of the songs Jim would be playing. He practiced diligently on a rented bass guitar as we drove to our Canadian destination. He had fifteen songs to learn, and he wasn't really a bass player. Certainly, he was a guitarist and a very good one, but a bass guitar is a totally different instrument and needs a different approach . . . a different mindset. Nevertheless, by the time we had reached the venue, Jim was showing his professionalism and had learned the basics of the tunes. We were able to catch a well-earned nap before that night's first show. Stage call was for eleven o'clock, and we all assembled in the dressing room at ten thirty. Everyone downed a few beers and, with plenty of Dutch courage, the band walked onstage. Nerves left after I played the opening few bars, and somehow or other we all struggled through the set, with the music sounding disjointed on occasion! By one o'clock in the morning, the ordeal was over, and back in the dressing room I felt relieved and actually quite pleased. I was also a little worried because the local newspaper reporter was there on assignment to review the performance for the morning edition. Needless to say, when I received the paper the next morning, I was apprehensive. I turned to the entertainment section, and there was a photograph of me onstage. The caption underneath stated, "New Savoy Brown lineup shines."

# CHAPTER 19

## HOLLYWOOD, A ROCK 'N' ROLL WARRIOR, AND I'M BROKE AND BUSTED

We keep moving forward, opening new doors, and doing new things, because we're curious and curiosity keeps leading us down new paths.

—Walt Disney

My connections with London and Harry had broken down completely. Originally, I naively thought it would be business as usual when I moved, but now Harry was in prison, and I knew I was on my own. Around this time, I found out, surprisingly, that no one had trademarked the band name, and that was the next thing I did. That certainly didn't say much for Harry's administrative ability.

At the same time, I also ended up hiring a new manager by the name of Ira Blacker. He had been my agent in the 1970s and was now living and managing acts out of Los Angeles. Ira took me on as a client, and I would make trips to the West Coast and stay with him and his wife in the Hollywood Hills. My confidence was low. Ira helped me put together a band of itinerant musicians, and a deal was made with a record label, Townhouse Records. The new band consisted of myself on guitar, Barry Paul on guitar, John Humphrey on bass, Keith Boyce on drums, and Ralph Morman on vocals. I made two albums for Townhouse, *Rock 'n' Roll Warriors* and a live double album, *Greatest Hits Live in Concert*.

That band also went on the road. The singer, Ralph Morman, was a great guy . . . until he drank. Then he became very difficult. I once stopped the bus, miffed over his drinking habit, and we both squared off on the highway.

"You're finished as a guitarist. You can't play anymore." Ralph's acid tongue cut deeply.

I put it down to the alcohol, but I knew there was a grain of truth to his words. Having Ralph in the band while he was drinking was an untenable situation until I thought we had found a solution. He promised me he'd be a good boy if we took his wife, Helen, on the road. Against my instincts, I agreed. It turned out that his wife was even worse than Ralph. Members of the band came up to me and asked me if I knew what was going on. I didn't know what they meant. They explained that Helen had been putting Ralph to bed and then trying to get cozy with the other band members. The end came when I got a call in the middle of the night and had to go to a local jail to get both of them released. They had been charged with disturbing the peace. I put Ralph and Helen on a Greyhound bus, said goodbye to them, and canceled the tour. During that time period, my guitar playing wasn't very good. In fact, I didn't even play on one of the band's releases. It was a commercial track, "Lay Back in the Arms of Someone." I had no feel for it. It was a pop song. Barry Paul, the second guitarist, played everything. It reached the Top 100 on the pop charts, the last single to chart, and I never even played on it. It stands as the only Savoy Brown song that I didn't play on.

The fact of the matter was that I wasn't in my element, and the whole put-together band situation in Los Angeles was collapsing. Before dysfunctionality led me to officially break up that band, Judas Priest invited me on their US national tour. They were hugely successful with radio mainstream hits at the time, and you would often see their videos on MTV. "Breaking the Law" was a powerful rebel-styled song that I liked. I had heard of the band in their early days, and I really liked their blues-based heavy-metal rock sound. More than anything, they had great songs and good guitar tones.

I wondered why I was added to the tour. It was a major event that year. I started to put the pieces together when guitarist K. K. Downing talked to me one day. "I used to see you at my local music hall back in the '60s," he said. I thought to myself that he might be a Flying V player, because he would have seen me playing one at that time. I was feeling very pleased with myself and starting to see myself as Mr. Cool. The conversation continued. "Yeah, I remember one of the times I saw you. I'll never forget it." I was getting even more pleased with myself.

Downing continued, "You were wearing cool clothes."

I was now relishing the memory. Then, the last thing he said was done with a twinkle in his eye. My ego was about to take a bruising. "Yeah, the night was unforgettable . . . the zipper in your pants was open the whole show."

Ira then came up with another game plan. He had the idea of forming a sort of supergroup that would consist of Tim Bogert on bass, Brian Auger on Hammond organ, Greg Errico on drums, and myself on guitar. It was a good plan, and it worked musically. Everyone played and sang. Each member played the songs they were known for. In my case, that was "Tell Mama" and "Hellbound Train," to name two of them. The personalities were strong, and it felt good for me not to be "the leader." I could sit back, relax, and just be one of the guys. We took that band on the road for a short tour, but it was quite obvious that the administration end of the deal, run by Ira, was a shambles. Seeing the writing on the wall, I quit the tour in New Orleans and drove home. I had had enough of Los Angeles and of everyone concerned. However, I did not make a principled exit, and Blacker sued me and took me into bankruptcy. His wife wrote to me much later on, after the two had separated, apologizing. I should have written back, but the experience was still a sore issue with me, and I never replied.

The 1980s had not started well for me. I packed my bags and said goodbye to Ira Blacker and Hollywood. I drove back to Ohio. Ira had sued me and won. I was bankrupt, my marriage fell apart, and, at that point, I was literally penniless. I moved to upstate New York. My tax returns for three years had a bunch of zeros on them. The only thing that kept me going was a small inheritance after my mother died. I managed a few thousand dollars very well. One chicken would last me a week. A musician friend sold me a car for $100. A girlfriend provided company, and bar owners let me drink for free. I slept on friends' couches. I had the best time of my life. I was free.

# CHAPTER 20

## CRESCENDO RECORDS, DAVE RETURNS . . . AND LEAVES

Success is walking from failure to failure
with no loss of enthusiasm.
—Winston Churchill

Following my awkward days in Los Angeles, I started going to see musician friends in Ithaca, New York. Eventually, in the mid-1980s, I moved to that area. I was coming off bankruptcy and the failed marriage and was sleeping on couches at the homes of musician pals. In Ithaca, I had no money and no guitar. I had nothing. My friends were members of the band the Rods, a heavy-metal group. I hung out at drummer Carl Cannedy's house and slept on bassist/vocalist Garry Bordonaro's couch. Garry had even sold me the hundred-dollar car. I got through that time period only because of Garry's support. Ithaca is considered to be the first Hollywood and is often referred to as the "Silent Hollywood." Films were first made there in the early 1900s. So, I exchanged the new Hollywood for an old Hollywood. It turned out to be an excellent time for me. I wasn't working, but I spent a summer discovering the many wonderful state parks in the area as well as the drinking holes.

Captain Jack's was the local bar at which to hang out. Many touring bands would play at that venue. Rick Nelson was there one night and Buddy Guy on another. I decided I had to see Buddy's show. Stevie Ray Vaughan had played at Cornell, the local university, that week, and a couple of thousand people had bought tickets. For the Buddy Guy show that same week, about thirty folks showed up. I was amazed at the low turnout, but that didn't matter. When I walked in and heard Buddy's voice, I thought the angels were singing. I watched the first two sets, and then the club owner talked to Buddy. I was invited onstage for the third set to jam on a song or two. I played very well, and afterward Buddy offered me a gig. I was embarrassed because I had my own career going, albeit in reverse gear, at that time and wasn't sure he even knew who I was. I ignored the offer, had a few drinks, and went my way.

Going my own way—or was it running away—had become a habit, whether it stemmed from business relationships or marriage. When things became unfixable, I preferred the outcome of letting the other person win. I always felt I could survive. I always had a belief in myself that things would work out. Even this time, I knew I still had my talent buried somewhere inside me. I was sure it would see me through.

It was at this time that I met Arnie Goodman. He was a record store owner and music lover, and he ended up taking care of business for me. In effect, he became my manager. Arnie was tall and slim. He had been a basketball player in college and also played in Italy before following his passion for music and opening successful stores in Brooklyn, New York. At first, it was thought by Arnie that I could be packaged toward the hard-rock market, and with that idea in mind, I put Savoy Brown on the shelf and formed the Kim Simmonds Band. I did some demos and gigs, but little came of it apart from making friends with those band members. Those friendships last until this day, particularly with guitarist "Duck" McDonald and singer Jimmy Kunes.

My mother's small inheritance had been a lifeline. I was broke. I found a furnished rental apartment and had a nice girlfriend, Shelly, who helped me through this time. Shelly was a stable influence, something I desperately needed. I was in an impoverished state, but that enabled me to have one of the best summers of my life. I realized I had nothing to lose. I had already lost it all. I found great joy in doing free things in life, such as going to the library and walking in a park. The local state park areas and lakes, of which there were many, were wonderful, and exploring them was something I really enjoyed. While I was enjoying life without much responsibility, the Kim Simmonds Band played some club gigs. The band never officially recorded and never quite got off the ground. It fizzled out. I never had the greatest confidence in the project, and that didn't help the situation. Manager Arnie suggested I bring vocalist Dave Walker back into the band. I took his advice, and once again Dave took on the Savoy Brown lead vocalist mantle. Arnie was the motivating factor in having Walker return. I had reservations at first, but it was a good idea. Dave had sung during my most-commercial successes, and he, too, had immigrated to the USA some years earlier to settle in Northern California. Arnie Goodman then orchestrated a record deal with the Los Angeles–based company Crescendo Records, and we were off and running. The band was completed with local musicians, drummer Al Macomber and bassist Jim Dagnesi. Eventually the band became a five-piece with Rick Jewett on the Hammond organ.

I went on to make three albums with Crescendo Records. They included *Make Me Sweat*, *Kings of Boogie*, and a live recording titled *Live and Kickin'*. I was songwriting fairly well. Producer Neil Norman was very encouraging. "You're a great blues-rock songwriter," he said. I needed to hear that.

I toured the band, crisscrossing the country many, many times. I now had moved to Elmira, New York, and was living in a house that Shelly had bought. I helped her get on her feet and was an encouragement to her. The relationship wasn't destined to last, but it was a benefit to both of us at a time when we both were finding our way.

I took the band to Europe and did my first tour of Spain. Getting to Spain wasn't without trepidation. We had flown from upstate New York to Kennedy Airport to catch our international flight across the Atlantic. All was going smoothly for the first half hour of the flight, until keyboardist Rick turned to me. "That doesn't look good," he said with humor.

I looked out the window in the direction his eyes were pointing. The engine was on fire! Simultaneously, the whole cabin got the message, and I have never heard an airplane so quiet before. No one was talking. All were in their own heads with their own thoughts. The captain came over the intercom with an announcement explaining the situation. Although it was a huge airplane, and we now had an engine on fire, he explained he could fly without the engine and that we were going to turn around and land back at Kennedy Airport. No one said a word on the return trip. As we approached the airport, I could see the ambulances and fire engines lined up along our intended runway. Rick's words ricocheted in my head: "This doesn't look good."

As we landed, the auxiliary emergency vehicles drove alongside us on the runway. Nothing bad happened. We slowed to a stop and made it back to the gate in one piece. Relieved, we deplaned in an orderly fashion. Once out of the plane, Rick and I ran as fast as we could to the bar!

I toured that band all over the fifty states, playing theaters, festivals, and small venues. Those latter venues, bars, really, always look and feel cold, and even depressing, when you are there in the daytime. However, when evening comes around and the lights are dimmed, everything begins to look warm and comforting. That's how the public sees things when they pay for their tickets and come to see a show. There's not much glamour at three o'clock in the afternoon. You see a cleaning person sweeping the kitchen and a few waitresses arranging tables. Often, the dressing rooms still have not been cleaned from the night before when you enter and sit down.

At one of those types of places, in the Midwest, during a tour that lasted a few weeks, I was sitting in a booth in the main room with Dave Walker. He was sharing his latest problem with me, and I looked at him as he spoke. He was wearing prescription sunglasses.

"I've got a loose cap on one of my front teeth," he said solemnly. "This morning it fell off, but I was able to find it on the bathroom floor." I looked at his mouth as he spoke, and there were no gaps. "Looking good now," I replied.

"Well, yeah, I stuck it back on with glue."

I was astonished. "Glue?!"

"Sure. I do it all the time. Saves going to the dentist. I may have to start using Super Glue, though."

As he was saying this, I was thinking about the downside of putting Super Glue in your mouth.

"Can you do that?" I asked.

"Why not?" was his reply.

Dave was a tough guy to begin with. He had been born and bred in the Midlands, England, and was rough around the edges. He had grown up during the immediate years after the Second World War and knew tough times. His cropped hair showed clear blue eyes, and his chin jutted out. Scars over both eyes were a testament to some fights he had been in . . . and won. He didn't so much as walk; he strutted with a swagger.

We finished talking, and I watched Dave walk away with his leather jacket worn casually off his shoulders and swinging loosely. He was a really good guy.

My road manager called me to the stage, and I tried out my guitar and amplifier, making sure it was working correctly. One of the tone knobs was crackling. Dirt and dust had to be clogging up a pot inside. So, we sprayed the inside pot with cleaner, and all was well. That was a minor problem. The not-so-minor problem was Dave's mood as I saw him walking around adjusting his front molar. He wasn't happy.

We had time to go back to the hotel before showtime, and that was always a plus. No one wanted to wait for hours before the show in a dingy dressing room. I took a short nap for five minutes. It was a knack I had developed quite early on after discovering the benefits of napping. It would always revive me. On other occasions, instead of sleeping, I would lie with my back on the floor and completely relax. That was another way for me to recharge. I had already been using that process to sleep at night and calm my mind since discovering yoga at sixteen years old. I couldn't get to sleep because I was constantly thinking of songs for the shows and how to fix a set list.

When we returned to the club, Dave had glued his cap on his front tooth, and all was set for the night's performance. He was okay with it, so I thought no more of it. The club had a small dance floor in front of the stage. By the time we were close to the end of the show, some people were really getting into the music and started whirling around in front of us. We were at a particular climax in one song when suddenly Dave jumped onto the dance floor and got down on his knees.

"Good move," I thought. "Get with the crowd."

It seemed as though Dave was being a great entertainer. It turns out that wasn't the case at all. He was looking for his tooth cap. It had worked itself loose and had fallen out! Pretty soon, part of the audience was also on their knees, trying to help find the missing cap, but to no avail. The band kept playing, and with an ugly gap in his teeth, Dave finished singing the song and we ended the show.

"We'll have to find a dentist," I said as we changed back into our street clothes.

Dave wasn't happy because that solution would take some time, and, meanwhile, he would look pretty bad chatting up the girls. We were ruminating on this whole predicament as we were just about to leave the club. A knock came on the door, and a big, burly biker walked in.

"Lost your tooth?" he asked flatly. "Well, I found it." He produced the small white object in his hand, and we were all really relieved.

"Where was it?" I asked.

"It was lodged in a corner of the dance floor," the biker replied. "I know what it's like to lose a tooth, and I wasn't going to let your guy be the same as me." With that, he opened his mouth and smiled . . . showing gums only. No front teeth!

Pittsburgh, Pennsylvania, was another date on that tour, and that city has always been good to me. I arrived at the venue with the band around five in the afternoon. It was a Friday, and the traffic had already been difficult. We were all a little frayed around the edges, and it hadn't even been that long of a drive. We had played in Cleveland the night before, and it was a drive of about three hours. Normally, drives between shows average about five hours, so this shorter trip was a welcome relief. In addition, the weather was cooperating. It was early spring, but more like winter on this day. Some vintage bands shy away from working during the deepest winter months if they can, and they take off from December until April or May. It's a good idea but, of course, there is no income.

I had played at this Pittsburgh venue before, so I knew Mario, the owner. At the time, he was "old" by my standards. I was in my thirties, and he was in his sixties. He would buy me a drink, and we'd sit and chat. As his name suggests, he was Italian, and I had a feeling he had connections with gangsters of the old school. He had thick hair, by now graying at the temples, and had a twinkle in his eye that was both mischievous and endearing. I've often wondered how some club owners, in a very difficult business, can be so happy and fun to be with. Most of the club venues I have played, certainly in the 1980s, are long gone, as is the one I'm talking about now. I was sad to see some of the clubs disappear, but had the feeling that I was glad to have outlived the bad ones. Perhaps one shouldn't harbor ill will, but we're all human.

So, this night in Pittsburgh was starting off on a good footing. I was drinking my classic Manhattan bourbon cocktail, and the artistic juices were beginning to come alive inside my brain and body. A Manhattan is a small drink, but it packs a punch. It's a sophisticated and strong way to start an evening. In the meantime, as Mario and I drank and talked, the crew had set up the equipment onstage, and everything was ready to go. My Marshall amplifier was stage right, my preferred place to stand. I finished my drink, excused myself, and got onstage for the sound check. I had a new road manager with me who thought he knew everything (he didn't last long), and he was busy stage managing. I started up a song with the band, and as we progressed with the tune, a few bikers walked in. They looked tough and I heard they were possibly part of the motorcycle gang The Drifters. I wasn't bothered, although there was tension in the air. In fact, after finishing the sound check, I sat down with the leader of the biker group and chatted. He wasn't the most sociable guy, but I was adept at dealing with all sorts of people after being on the road, even at that time, for a couple of decades. For instance, most nights I'd have some overly drunk fans wanting to hang out with me. Sometimes, they might veer on being abusive, and I would gently pull them back to civility. I could handle drunks, so I thought I could also manage a gang leader. All went well and we talked. His leather jacket was studded and seemed a size too big. It hung loosely over his shoulders. He had shoulder-length hair that was unkempt, and he carried a furtive look in his eyes.

He asked, "Will you be playing 'Hellbound Train' tonight?" His words had a hollowness to them, as if they were dead on arrival.

"I usually play it," I replied. "I'll do it, for you, for sure."

I smiled, but he wasn't buying my act. That was it. I didn't think any more of the conversation until the end of the night. The dressing room was in an odd place and quite small. You had to access it via an outside steel staircase that led to the top of the old building. It was uncomfortable, but in those days I easily got around that problem by downing a couple of beers. The green room had a supply of alcohol, and that was always good fuel for a two-hour show. American club venues don't often provide the same hospitality as their European counterparts. With the latter, besides beer, a special chef often cooks the evening meal, and there are always sandwiches, desserts, local-area treats, and some fine wine. In Pittsburgh that night, it was Budweiser Light.

I changed into a dress shirt, pressed slacks, and a showy jacket that had colorful butterfly images hand-stitched into the cloth. The jacket had a sheen to it that was formal in a rock-and-roll way. I always dressed for the stage, and I've never understood the value of looking like a slob in front of an audience paying to see you perform. Lots of musicians underdress, especially in these more-casual times. I like to put pressure on myself by dressing up. Dressing down, intentionally, can be a stress reliever . . . maybe.

It was 10:00 p.m. and time to go on. In the 1980s, clubs were way behind the times. The audience for my kind of music was getting older and didn't want to stay at a club until one in the morning. They wanted an early show so they could get home early and look forward to a good night's sleep before work the next morning. But club owners and managers insisted on bands starting late. The earliest would have been 10:00 p.m. Of course, the longer they could keep people drinking at the bar, the better the profits. This particular night, the waitresses were working overtime. I had an audience that liked to "party."

The show started on time. There was little fanfare. I counted the band in, and we started rocking. We played a two-hour set, and at the end of the show, it was time for the song "Hellbound Train." As soon as the drummer played the intro, all hell broke loose in front of the bandstand. Apparently, a rival gang had arrived, and my song triggered their bitter hostility toward each other. There was no fighting, but there was GOING to be a fight. You could sense the atmosphere change. We finished the set, and the bikers were now outside, and we could hear some kind of commotion. It was a smallish venue, and the exits weren't far away from the stage. The police arrived, and that's when things got nasty. Suddenly, Mario hustled us upstairs to the dressing room. "Stay here," he commanded.

Our new road manager arrived, quite ashen faced: "They're shooting at each other. They've drawn guns!"

A firefight had started outside the club. We had no idea what to do, so we stayed put until the whole affair died down. It was 2:00 a.m. by the time we were finally able to exit the dressing room. The police had managed the situation well, and no one, gang members or police, had been shot or injured.

All was clear. I had changed into my street clothes. As I got on the bus to leave for the hotel, as everyone was talking about the craziness that night, out of the shadows stepped the gang leader I had spoken with earlier. His jacket had the words "The Drifters," along with a skull, stitched into the black leather. I hadn't noticed the jacket details earlier. He looked darkly at me, pulled out a small cheroot, and lit it. He puffed smoke circles into the air as he looked around, checking his boundaries. A couple of his rider pals stood off to the side. He looked back into my eyes and was staring menacingly. I was worried now. Then he said, "I wanted to stick around. I've got to tell you. That was the best version of "Hellbound Train" you've ever played. Thanks, man. See you next time."

I had now reached my forties and was not making much of a substantial living. The band's growth had begun to stall. Dave Walker left me a second time and went back to living outside the music business in his new home in the state of New Mexico. He finally settled in Colorado, where he continued to avoid the music business apart from singing locally.

I parted ways with Arnie, but he has remained one of my closest friends to this day and has continued to help me from afar in a consultancy way. In fact, he was the catalyst for putting me together with my current record label, Quarto Valley Records (QVR). Dave Walker was now gone for good from the Savoy Brown family. I looked around to see what direction I should take. I needed a singer first and foremost.

Next, I was to meet Debbie, my lifelong partner, and everything would change dramatically for the better. My dad had been right. You can start life again in your forties.

# CHAPTER 21

## DEBBIE ENTERS MY LIFE, CENTRAL NEW YORK, AND THE BLUES KEEP ME HOLDING ON

You have to be fast on your feet and adaptive or else a strategy is useless.

—Charles de Gaulle

While based in central New York, I met Debbie, and she would eventually become my third wife and lifelong partner. She was the special woman I had looked for all my life. Her red hair was the first thing I noticed when we met at a local club in Syracuse. Her petite body was also a nice physical attraction. However, more than that, deep down, I knew she was the one for me . . . beyond looks.

She could look haughty, she could be very vulnerable, and she could be supersweet, but she couldn't be pushed around. She's wonderful at making a house a home, she's never let us carry any debt, and she has supported me unwaveringly. Her most amazing trait is that she never complains!

More than anything, our values were the same and we just clicked. Debbie never talks about politics or religion, and we never argue about money. I believe that all of that is a blessing. Many marriages have failed on one of those accounts. I fell madly in love with her, and we settled down together in her hometown in central New York, about five hours from New York City.

Debbie was a great help to me, to say the least, including suggestions as to how I was running the band. In effect, she became my personal manager.

I started taking charge of the business side of things instead of letting others do it. Debbie also worked in that area. For instance, we stopped renting touring vehicles and, instead, bought them ourselves to save a lot of money. She was also the catalyst for me to stop drinking alcohol, a habit of mine that had gotten out of control.

By now, I knew more about life and the music business than almost anyone I knew, so it seemed natural for me to run the show. Debbie was involved with every one of my decisions as we moved forward, and I had the ultimate veto power. She allowed me to make many mistakes and continue in my own impetuous way, but she always had a firm hand on the finances. There would be no more crashing and burning along the way!

While she looked after our bank accounts, organized all aspects of my life, and kept me sober, she let me run the band. I was finally growing up. I was in a domestic situation that was solid. That was something I had wanted all my life, and it gave me a base to start making good decisions. I was handling the band myself, for better or for worse.

I was finally getting by in a rational manner. I had a furnished apartment. I had my health. I still had my boyish looks. I was still enthusiastic about life. I had also stopped drinking, and that was a major move. My relationship with Debbie had been the catalyst. I didn't want to lose her through destructive behavior, so I stopped, cold turkey, with no twelve-step program. I did drink nonalcoholic beer to trick my mind into thinking I was getting alcohol. I counted each hour I hadn't taken a drink. Then, I counted each day, each week, each year, until two or three years had gone by and I was free of alcohol. Now, it's been decades, and I've stopped counting. It's life-changing when you stop drinking. Most of us cross those kinds of bridges in life only when we absolutely HAVE to. We hang on to bad habits as long as possible. Becoming teetotal by simply stopping, I showed myself I had willpower. It's not something I've ever publicized, but it is a big deal.

I bought a new home with Debbie, and we started a family. We were living in a home purchased from Debbie's sister, Sharon. She was selling the house to live with her new husband, Dennis, in his home. Buying a home without a bank loan was a perfect way to become a homeowner again. Instead, we paid Sharon, and she held the "mortgage."

Debbie and I had the same values, and it's those values, when aligned, that are the key to a relationship that lasts. Our daughter, Eve, was soon born, and the stage was set for decades to come. Debbie was looking after the house, the bills, and everything connected to the home. Effectively, that left me free to be an artist, play guitar, write songs, and tour.

Eventually, as my career became stable again, we built a custom home on our plot of land. It is a piece of property that's been in Debbie's family for years. She designed it, took care of all the practical issues, arranged for the building contractors, and got it all done while I gallivanted around the country playing music. Debbie grew up in the home next door, which her parents had built themselves. Her grandmother had a home where our garage now stands, so the land we live on has quite the family roots underneath and around it.

The support I received from Debbie's parents, Marj and Jerry, was amazing. They lived a quarter mile down the road but never interfered. In addition, they were always there to lend a helping hand. Marj came from a family of fourteen, and I loved talking to her about those days in America when those large families all lived and worked on a family farm. It was a time we'll never see again, and she was my window into that glorious past. She had tragedy in her life when her first husband, and Debbie's dad, had died in a work accident. Each year, we would go to his grave and place flowers in remembrance. Marj and Jerry are next to that same plot now. Jerry had become a second father to me. He would constantly help me with house repairs, and we became golfing partners. My personal life was at a level of success I had always wanted but never achieved before. I could tour knowing I had a solid homelife waiting for me to return.

Syracuse, New York, was the closest big city to me, and I befriended producer Greg Spencer. He was also the owner of Blue Wave Records. Now that Dave Walker had left the band again, I didn't have a singer. Greg produced the Savoy Brown album *Let It Ride* in 1992. It featured three guest vocalists, Pete McMahon, Joe Whiting, and Phil McDonald. I also sang one song called "Down All the Days." It was an acoustic song, and I found I could sing in a low register and be effective. I heard someone say that I'd be a good country singer after that vocal was completed. The song itself reflected the many down periods I had experienced during the previous decade.

I was making many acquaintances in and around Syracuse. I realized, with the help of Debbie by my side, that my life was now happier than at any other time in my life. At Greg Spencer's suggestion, I asked Pete

McMahon to be my singer. Pete also played harmonica, and he was great at both. Greg had recorded Pete with his own band, the Kingsnakes. I was forming a nucleus of friends who all knew each other well. Pete always wore a beret in the usual bluesman fashion. In his case, it was to hide a thinning head of hair. He was photogenic and a musician with deep blues roots. He had a cool demeanor and an attractive, lazy way of talking. His voice was deep and often reminded me of John Lee Hooker. In fact, Pete had worked with Hooker and knew him well. It was good for me to work with Pete. He was someone who understood the music I grew up with.

Initially, I added two musicians, Andy Ramirez and Joe Pierloni, from Rochester, New York. However, fairly quickly, I changed to more-experienced players, bassist Jim Heyl and Dave Olson, a former drummer for Robert Cray. I was off and running, with agents in San Francisco booking me and independent record labels knocking on my door.

When it came to recording my next album, *Bring It Home*, Arnie Goodman came back into my life. Arnie had sold his record stores and was moving in a new direction within the music business. He had started Viceroy Records. The album is a fine recording, with songs of mine, songs written with Pete, and a couple of cover tunes. "Too Much of a Good Thing" is a blues shuffle-style song that I'm proud of. "Too much of a good thing going on last night" was the punch line.

One of my favorite blues musicians from the generation before me, Hubert Sumlin, guested on a track. Hubert had been Howlin' Wolf's guitarist, so I did the Wolf song "Shake for Me" so that Hubert would be on familiar ground. Hubert was a sweetheart. I also invited Dave Peverett along to sing my song "High on Your Love." Dave and I had become good friends again. After I let him go from Savoy Brown and after the huge success of his own band, Foghat, the circle had turned, and we both were together as we had been before any of our musical journeys had begun.

*Bring It Home* was recorded at Ben Elliot's Showplace Studios in New Jersey. The studio was part of a one-story building that also housed a gentleman's club . . . okay, a strip club. One afternoon, Pete and I took a break, and we started exploring the various studio rooms we weren't using. One room we hadn't looked into had an unusual door. I tried it, and it opened easily. Inside, it was dark and there was a corridor. I could hear sounds at the other end. Pete and I decided to check things out. We walked to the end of the corridor and found ourselves in the strip club. Surprise! Once the roadies found out that little secret, they were over in the strip club relaxing during each break moment. As time went on, they started bringing the Russian strippers over to the studio to impress them. The girls were beautiful, but it had to be stopped. We were working and didn't need any other distractions while we were learning the songs!

I used my Les Paul and a Marshall amplifier on *Bring It Home* and got a very good tone in the process. I was now getting back to my best playing again. Pete McMahon helped because he was steeped in the blues, and I finally had someone in my band that knew the blues inside and out and wasn't simply a rock and roller who could play the blues. It helped as well that Dave Olson was also a great blues drummer. Dave was a founding member of the Robert Cray Band, so he had mountains of experience and knowledge. Bassist Jim Heyl was also the perfect musical addition and brought a positive and happy outlook to the band. An altogether good guy.

*Bring It Home* doesn't get enough attention and is now an item buried in the catalog, but some consider it to be one of the best Savoy Brown recordings. I'm looking forward to a time in the future when it gets rediscovered. I hope that's sooner than later, so I can enjoy the moment.

After touring to support the album for a couple of years, Dave Olsen retired from show business. Pete decided to roll on with a solo career, and Jim and I simply drifted off in our separate ways. Nothing stays the same.

At this point in time, with Greg Spencer's help, and a feeling I wasn't getting any younger, I began to think about what other musical options I might have available to me. I thought of the idea of making a solo acoustic album. I had recorded an album in that fashion earlier but hadn't taken it seriously as a career move.

Taking a more professional look at an acoustic side of myself, I thought I would tour in support of the album with just an acoustic guitar and myself playing and singing. It would help develop my singing and my performance ability and give me a break from bandleading.

The album that came out of all this, produced by Greg and released on his Blue Wave records label, was *Solitaire*. The year was 1997, and I followed the release by gigging at small venues. It was an enormous benefit to me. I found myself onstage playing an acoustic guitar (quite the challenge for an electric player) and having to sing with very little enhancement. I was also learning to communicate with a small crowd via storytelling and banter between songs. When you do those kinds of solo shows, you have to think on your feet, so to speak.

In my case, I had a set list, but in order to make the show flow and work for the audience, I had to be ready to change a song at any point or make a quick turn in the musical approach if I thought something wasn't working. I also found myself in environments I wouldn't be in with the band. I played some small folk clubs and house parties. When I did play in theaters, I had to put enormous energy into my performances so that the larger areas didn't swallow up a solo act.

In all, I ultimately recorded five solo acoustic albums, culminating in 2015 with *Jazzin' on the Blues*, an all-instrumental guitar album in which I also played bass and harmonica. Ron Keck played percussion. I released it on my own record label, Panache Records. I didn't tour with that release. By then, I think I realized it was just fun to express myself in different ways in the studio, but that it could be left at that.

The band was still my priority, and although Arnie Goodman didn't play a part in the *Solitaire* album, he nevertheless continued with me in his usual roving consultant role. He set up my next recording venture. He suggested Nathaniel Peterson to me as a replacement vocalist and bass player after Pete, Dave, and Jim had gone their separate ways. Nathaniel played bass and sang. I was able to continue simply as a three-piece with him, and he was a terrific blues singer and musician. He was a big and tall man who had served in the military. He was a Black American from Detroit and was cosmic in personality. His cheek was tattooed, and he looked ferocious but was quite the opposite. He was charming and without malice.

A few drummers worked with Nathaniel and me. T (Thomas) Xiques was first, and he was a young man who had gone to the Berklee College of Music. He told me he thought Berklee had ruined him because of the technical standard of many of the other students.

Drummer Al Kash was almost my age and a wonderful, tall, and lanky individual. He had spent part of his life in Australia after being raised in Florida. My hectic tour schedule, crisscrossing America, was the primary reason for Al leaving, and T had other offers he wanted to pursue.

The absolute right drummer for me at the time was Tom Compton. Tom had played for years with Alvin Lee and then for more than a decade with Johnny Winter. Now, that's a pedigree and a wealth of experience. I loved playing with Tom and Nathaniel. It was the band I could take into the studio with confidence. The studio, again, was Ben Elliott's Showplace Studios, where we recorded *The Blues Keep Me Holding On*.

We had first rehearsed at my own studio. That is the studio I call the "White Cottage Studio," and it has a very interesting history. One day, Debbie and I were driving in the rural area in which we live. Suddenly, Debbie pointed out a building in a field. "That's cool," she said. "That would make a nice guesthouse. I wonder who owns it."

We found the owner. The building had been owned by a woodworker. We purchased it for $2,000 and then had to solve the problem of how to have it transported to our backyard. We selected a spot about 30 yards from my house as the site for the cottage, and a concrete base was constructed. Debbie then hired a flatbed truck to pick up the building and bring it to us. That was quite involved, since we had to get permission from various government offices. We had to find a route that avoided power lines and other obstacles, so the truck with the building on the back could get to us unimpeded. We succeeded, and the building was set on its base. The A-frame inner ceiling had been lowered for transport and was raised again by Jerry. He then put on a new tiled roof for me. Other family members helped with electric lines and such. There was much more interior work to be done, mostly by Jerry's hand. The plans to turn it into a guesthouse soon became plans to make it a rehearsal room, and then, by extension, a full-blown one-room recording studio. I had hijacked Debbie's great guesthouse idea, a situation I wouldn't have had the imagination to see.

So, Nathaniel, Tom, and I rehearsed and recorded demos for *The Blues Keep Me Holding On* in the White Cottage Studio. Ben Elliott remarked to me that it was a good-sounding studio. I am an early-morning person, and I always like to start recording at 10:00 a.m. That's not always possible, but in a perfect world, 10:00 a.m. works for me. That's how I started for the first album back in 1967 at Decca Records. Mike Vernon had us begin each day at ten. It worked, and I've kept that routine ever since. *The Blues Keep Me Holding On* was excellent, but the record label was an independent label, and they didn't seem to get the word out. They didn't seem to know what to do with the product once they had it in their hands!

There is one story from that session. We arrived at the studio the night before the sessions were to begin, to set up our equipment and be ready to go the next day. I placed my Les Paul guitar on a guitar stand. An assistant engineer walked by and knocked the guitar off its stand. The neck of the guitar broke off cleanly. Catastrophe! I wouldn't be using that guitar, and I had no other guitar apart from a slide guitar, which would not fit the role as a solo instrument to cover all the material. The solution was for my tour manager Bob Golino to drive overnight, back to my house, to pick up a Gibson 335 guitar that I figured would get me a similar sound as my Les Paul. Bob was able to make the almost nine-hour round trip and get back in time for the beginning session the next day. The sessions did begin at 10:00 a.m. that day. It was an amazing piece of driving and sacrifice by Bob.

After the album was recorded, the usual milieu of gigs and more gigs followed. For years at this time, for most of the gigs, I had traveled by road and often did my own driving. I enjoyed the trips. I enjoyed seeing the sights of America. I have also especially liked Florida, like so many Britishers, because tropical weather has a major appeal after growing up on the damp island of Great Britain. The western states of Wyoming, Arizona, and Oregon are also beautiful to drive through. I've often wondered what real need there is to travel the world. We have it all here in the USA. I've been to parts of Spain, and you'd think it was Arizona. Connecticut and Vermont are reminiscent of old England. Welsh-like towns can be found in Pennsylvania. On the road, as much as I enjoyed life, it could be difficult to handle. I had to cut corners and would often stay at cheaper hotels to keep to a budget. The venues were often small and challenging. At those times, when I was disgusted with what I was doing, I could call Debbie, and she would listen to me moan and complain. She always made me feel better about myself and the situation I found myself in.

Eventually, my relationship with Nathaniel came to an end. It seemed he wanted to move into a heavier rock direction, and a promoter in Italy helped him start a new career in that direction. He changed his name to Azariah Cain and continued on his cosmic journey. He was a personality that once you met him, you'd never forget him. Tom also parted company with me. He had never been too happy with the often-grueling schedule.

I continued to tour, and I was working with agent Bruce Solar, who had his own agency in San Francisco. The new millennium was approaching. I still had loads of energy and was considered a road warrior. I knew that people were saying things such as "How does he do it?" and "Where does he get the energy from?"

I was now approaching my sixtieth year. Could I keep going?

# CHAPTER 22

## THE NEW MILLENNIUM AND I SING

If a man does not keep pace with his companions, perhaps it is because he hears a different drummer. Let him step to the music which he hears, however, measured or far away.

—Henry David Thoreau

Life with Debbie was paying off in so many ways, and with Nathaniel gone, I looked at what my opportunities were going forward with the band. I had previously gotten to know Dave Malachowski from doing some local gigs around the Albany area. I knew he was a good guitarist. We met for lunch and got to know one another. This was at the end of the 1990s, and we laid out a plan that made him the bandleader while I simply became "the Artist." That was, at least, the plan put forward by Dave. He had played a similar dual role at the beginning of Shania Twain's career as a guitarist and bandleader. We thought that blueprint could work for me and the band. Dave had long, straight hair to his shoulders, was thin in build, and carried a sophisticated attitude. He had cut his teeth around the Boston rock scene and then settled in Woodstock, New York, which was not terribly far from me.

Dave brought in various musicians for auditions, and nothing seemed to work out. He then suggested a singer to me, but that singer needed quite a bit of coaching. I wasn't up to doing that task. I was fed up working with vocalists to understand their strengths and limitations. I was also fed up with having to pick the right songs and keys to suit them and to make sure they were front and center.

The situation convinced me, for a second time in my career, to take over the job as lead vocalist. Dave was on board with the plan. Dennis Cotton came into the band as the drummer, and Gerry Sorrentino came aboard as the bass player. This band configuration went forward and produced two albums. *Strange Dreams* was the studio album that was recorded in my own White Cottage Studio. The other, a live album, was recorded in Vancouver in Canada. We called it *You Should Have Been There*.

Drummer Dennis was prematurely bald and instantly likable. He had great social skills and was effervescent, the kind of guy who wanted to do anything asked of him. He laughed a lot and often stood up to me and my pessimistic attitude toward life. I appreciated him greatly, and he eventually started his own merchandise company producing Savoy Brown T-shirts of his own design.

Bassist Gerry was into bodybuilding. He had a sculpted figure from hours of being in the gym. He was 6 feet tall and seemed to understand me enough to put up with my foibles. Both Dennis and Gerry have remained lifelong friends even after we stopped working together.

Everything was now purring along like a well-tuned engine. I started my own record company called Panache Records and released the live album *You Should Have Been There* on my own label. I leased *Strange Dreams* to Blind Pig Records. From this point on, I was determined to produce and own all my own recordings. Along with Debbie, I was now my own manager and my own producer.

Putting new band lineups together always rejuvenated and excited me. It wasn't a drag. I was still young and in my fifties. I was still doing much of the driving to gigs. I had energy.

I did have a contentious relationship with Dave, and it was no surprise to anyone that we eventually parted company. Dave left the band in late June 2005, just before we were to play a house party. A fan of the band since the late 1960s, John Shelmet had discussed with me the possibility of the band playing at his home. It turned out to be a joint fiftieth birthday party for John and his wife, Billie Jo. We played the gig as a three-piece in Dave's absence, and it was quite the affair. They had the full production in the backyard, including lights and sound. It was a huge hit, and John stayed in touch, and we gradually became friends. John is a physician, and his love of music has always been a major way of coping with the stresses of practicing medicine. He became a sounding board for me when I needed input on the songs I was writing. For years now, he has been the first person to hear all of my music demos. His knowledge of Savoy Brown and my guitar playing has been invaluable to me when I need feedback to help chart a course for myself and the band. In addition to his musical input, he took on the job as the administrator of the Savoy Brown Facebook site. He is known as "the Savoy Brown Facebook Guy."

The band lineup that played John's party split up after six years or so. Dennis left the band to concentrate on his family and teaching. Mario Staiano, a friend of Gerry's, replaced Dennis on drums. For the second time in all the years, I continued on with a three-piece band. I discovered that Mario and I had similar personalities. He was small in stature, a New Yorker through and through, and he played the drums like a bull. The three of us recorded a new album in my studio, and it was released in 2007 on Panache Records. I gave the album the title *Steel*. I thought it reflected what you needed to be made of to survive in the music business. *Steel* was a difficult album for me to complete because once the basic drum and bass tracks were laid down, I was on my own in my studio without someone to help and give me input. That is the one thing about producing yourself. It may be fine with someone of my experience and ability, but I wouldn't recommend it to others.

The new millennium was moving along. Before I knew it, it was almost 2010. Pat DeSalvo had replaced Gerry on bass, and Garnet Grimm replaced Mario on drums. For many years, the band consisted of musicians who came from afar. For instance, Nathaniel would always fly in from where he lived near Palm Springs in California. The closest anyone lived to me was often a five-hour drive away. It made rehearsals difficult, and the travel put a strain on all involved. However, Pat and Garnet lived in my area, and they brought convenience to the situation in addition to being the right fit musically. Their membership in the band meant I could practice the band at will, since only a short drive separated us all. I now seemed committed to a three-piece band, and it was certainly easier to manage, not only because of it just being three people but also because of Pat's and Garnet's personalities.

Pat is of Italian descent and grew up in an Italian community. He has a stocky build with a dash of devil-may-care attitude in him. He has an amazing work ethic; he's a team player, and he's a musician who plays his instrument with great personality and ability. We actually had worked together years before he joined the band. He played stand-up bass during some of the sessions while I was recording some of my solo acoustic albums. Therefore, we knew each other and stayed in touch through the years before he became a band member. Pat started off having a great head of black hair, but now, after more than ten years of being in my band and putting up with me, his hair has turned gray!

Garnet is tall with wispy hair and carries a mild manner. He has a temper, as we all do, but I see very little of that. He served in the US Army, and that has given him very good discipline along with a Catholic school upbringing. He has a pleasant face and is very conscious of others' feelings. He would have made a very good record producer because of his calm way of analyzing problems. Musically, he plays a blues shuffle as well as anyone I've ever worked with or, indeed, anyone else in the world.

In total, Pat and Garnet have been behind me and Debbie every step of the way. They've always put me front and center. In return, I've built the band up around their talents, and they are members of the longest-running Savoy Brown lineup ever. It meant a long relationship, great musical chemistry, and a number of well-regarded blues albums (including a #1) along the way. When we started gigging, we were simply the three-piece with me singing. The great musical chemistry was apparent, but, being my restless self, I decided on adding a fourth member. My vocals had limitations, and I thought I'd take one more shot with another band singer. I had been a friend and business associate of Greg Spencer's since my first acoustic solo album in 1997. As the year 2011 beckoned, I started to think I needed a front man and lead singer again. It had been more than ten years since I had taken the lead in fronting the band and singing. Greg suggested Joe Whiting, a local Syracuse, New York, legend. Joe had previously sung in a local band I had put together as a side project a few years earlier. It had been known as "the Kim Simmonds Blues Express." It had been a lot of fun, even though the gigs were restricted to local bars and such in the central New York area. I asked Joe to join, and he jumped at the chance. A record deal was secured with Ruf Records, a German company known for its strong blues-rock music presence. I made the album *Voodoo Moon*. I used my own studio again, and the album was leased to Ruf Records, in keeping with my new business model. The company, led by Thomas Ruf, did an excellent job at promotion, and I took the four-piece band to Europe and around the States. We even went as far as Brazil and some of the Eastern Bloc European countries.

There were a good couple of years with Joe singing, and that culminated in a live album for Ruf Records titled *Songs from the Road*, which was recorded in Dortmund, Germany. Joe subsequently left the band and returned to his solo career at that point.

It was an interesting and successful couple of years as a four-piece band, but I had the lingering thought that the band chemistry, musically, was stronger as a three-piece. Therefore, I took my place again as the lead singer and front man while retaining Pat and Garnet as the rhythm section. There was, indeed, chemistry. We have now been together, as of this writing, for more than twelve years. In that period, seven albums were released, two of them live and five in the studio. *Goin' to the Delta* was first. That was a "back to the basics" blues/rock album recorded at SubCat Studios in Syracuse, New York. I followed that with *The Devil to Pay*. Both albums charted on the Billboard Blues Charts, but then my health took a turn for the worse . . . the very worse.

It started with a lump on the side of my neck. It ended with a seven-hour operation for cancer of my tonsils via robot technology. My CT scan was negative, to everyone's surprise. However, my experienced surgeon thought otherwise, and he strongly believed I did have tonsillar cancer despite the negative scan. I went under the knife, and cancer was confirmed. Postsurgery, I awoke to fairly good news from an assistant. It had been caught in time, and, in my case, there was a 90 percent chance for recovery. At this time, I'm a year past the five-year "all clear" sign.

When I was first diagnosed, I was more intrigued than scared. I knew, from the treatment options presented to me by the surgeon, that the surgical approach would involve a lot of pain. I had never experienced real pain before, and that was the intriguing part. What would be my capacity for pain? I chose the surgical option, and I wouldn't want to go through that again. The following radiation therapy wasn't as bad, although it severely impacted my sense of taste for quite a while. The immediate aftermath of the operation and the pain pills I had to take were the most-difficult things to get through. The inability to sleep properly, nausea, and, well, the pain was . . . a pain in the neck! It was just as difficult for my wife, Debbie. She was, at times, at a loss as to how she could help. The fact was that no one could help. You're simply on your own in many ways. Of course, Debbie WAS a great help, but it was hard for both of us to get through the immediate few weeks after the operation.

I did not have to have chemotherapy but did undergo a course of radiation. Radiation and the type of surgical approach were done so that my vocal cords would be unaffected. I came out of the whole episode as well as one might expect. Now, I am left with a residual feeling that the left side of my neck has been injected with Novocain, but I can live with that. It's no different than living with tinnitus in my ears. As with so much in my life, I simply ignore it. The bout with cancer left me with a feeling that I'd better get things done now and not coast along as if I had years of living guaranteed to me. It made me focus, and I began working on the third album with Pat and Garnet as a three-piece; *Witchy Feelin'* reached #1 on the Billboard Blues Chart. It was my first number one.

The reviews, comments, and feedback on *Witchy Feelin'* were amazing. We had knocked it out of the park. Savoy Brown, with Pat and Garnet, never sounded better. It was agreed the album was as good as anything from the 1960s. Many things contributed to the huge success of *Witchy Feelin'*. Thomas Ruf of Ruf Records had a strong presence in the blues community. Pat's and Garnet's input was invaluable. John Shelmet worked with me through the initial song selections and further evolution of several of the songs. I had also decided to take *Witchy Feelin'* back to Ben Elliott at Showplace Studios in New Jersey (I had recorded there in the 1990s), and that was a massive contribution to the success. Last, but not least, was my wife, Debbie, overseeing and organizing the whole project.

Now, how was I to follow that up? Quarto Valley Records (QVR Records) stepped into the picture and offered me a deal I couldn't refuse. Brokered by my old friend Arnie Goodman, QVR took me on, and I licensed them the 2019 *City Night* album. This was also recorded with Ben Elliott at his New Jersey studio. *City Night* reached #4 on the Billboard Blues Chart and got even more accolades. Owner Bruce Quarto is a marvelously energetic man, and he has Mike Carden to run the company. Both have become great friends, and I feel like part of a family with them.

With a new record label, I was still on the road, still with energy left, and looking forward to the next round of fighting in life and in the music business.

# AFTERWORD

The real glory is being knocked to your knees and then coming back. That's real glory. That's the essence of it.

—Vince Lombardi

My relationship with Bruce Quarto and Mike Carden continued, and after a great year of touring in 2019 through early February 2020, I decided a break of a couple of months would be good for the band. We would start again in the spring and pick up where we left off.

I had written material for a new album, but I was second-guessing myself on the songs and generally procrastinating about going into the studio. Ben Elliott changed all that. He encouraged me to record as quickly as possible. On his advice, I took the band to New Jersey, and a new release was begun. By now, I had worked with Ben on and off for countless years, so the process was fairly typical. Set up equipment, play live, and then overdub the vocals and lead guitar. That is it in a nutshell. I used my stage amplifier setup, and everything went smoothly.

I even had a song that turned out to be a great album title for *Ain't Done Yet*. That seemed to sum up where the band and I were at in life. Very shortly after the album was recorded, the COVID-19 pandemic hit, and I ended up doing one gig in two years. The rest of the time was spent at home either in lockdown or simply for general health and safety. Oh, and by the way, I also had a mild heart attack. An emergency hospital visit and one coronary artery stent later, I was back on my feet.

Luckily, thanks to Ben, I had finished the *Ain't Done Yet* album prior to the lockdown, and it was released in 2020. The interviews and such kept me going that year. I even did some music videos to promote the album, and they helped keep my spirits up. The album placed in the top five on the Billboard Blues Chart, and so the band rolled on . . . at least out there in the internet world.

Many people have said over the recent (and not so recent) years, "You should write a book." It has taken me a long time to finally do it. I had to feel I was at the right age, and also that I was in the right state of mind to address the past and take a long look at my life and career.

Certainly, the downtime in my life caused by COVID and lack of touring has played a part in me getting down my curious odyssey through life. I could have almost died many times along the way. There was the swimming pool incident and the time I was sick in the hospital when I was a child. There have been numerous near car crashes on the highway, and there was cancer. There was the time I was on an airplane turning around over the Atlantic and landing on one engine, and a plane turning around over the Rockies and landing safely after not being able to gain height. There was the time I fell asleep at the wheel while driving the band van at three in the morning, and the many skids and slides on icy winter roads and miraculous escapes.

I didn't mention the nearly vertical takeoff in a plane during an Alaskan wind-, snow-, and rainstorm. I also left out the six or seven deer I have hit traveling country roads to gigs, the countless bouts of food poisoning, having the flu or bronchitis, or the cuts and bruises, but still having to perform.

They say the show must go on . . . and it has. As Ray Charles once said, "Don't go backward; you've already been there."

After all is said and done, there's one thing I do know . . . music makes all our lives a little sweeter.

# EPILOGUES

## Debbie Lyons Simmonds

In August 2021, Kim was diagnosed with colon cancer. It was a very rare form that affects 1 percent of those who get diagnosed with it—even in illness, my husband was unique. He endured many rounds of chemotherapy (without complaint, I might add) from that time up until his passing in December 2022. I am grateful to say that Eve, our daughter, and I were at his side when the time came. Thank you to all the doctors, nurses, and staff who made things as easy as possible.

A side effect of the chemotherapy was peripheral neuropathy, which affected his hands and feet, making it hard for him to do the things he loved most—playing guitar and painting. I bring this up because the writing of this book ends, what some may say, abruptly. Some may see this as a symptom of the adversity Kim was facing during this time, though the book was in the works for a long time before he was diagnosed. If anything, it encouraged him to finish it—and that he did. He presented this to me as the completed version of the book, and introducing anything additional would not be true to his intentions.

I'm sure many of you are not aware that the last record, *Blues All Around*, was recorded after his diagnosis and while he was going through treatment. My husband was not about to let something like cancer get in the way of making music! I am so grateful to his steadfast bandmates Pat DeSalvo and Garnet Grimm for seeing the project through with him, and also to his friend and sounding board, John Shelmet, for all the help and advice he offered.

Getting the book to a publisher was no easy task. We had always been in the music business, not the book business—very different endeavors. Our dear friend Tony Bullard had spoken to both Kim and me on numerous occasions about getting the book out, but we just didn't know where to turn. In the summer of 2024, Tony received a text that included an excerpt from a book, *Fleetwood Mac in Chicago: The Legendary Chess Blues Session, January 4, 1969*, with the piece that Kim had written for the book. A lightbulb went on in Tony's head (but not mine, I'm sorry to say!). The book had been coauthored by Robert Schaffner, whom we had spoken with at a recent show, and as it turned out, Kim had met and connected with in the '70s. Small world. Tony asked if I knew him, was he still alive, and did I know how to reach him? I said yes to all! Tony made the call to Robert, who then connected me to Schiffer Publishing, and the result is what you're reading now. Needless to say, I am eternally grateful for Tony, who made the connection for me, and Robert, who has been an enormous help in putting this all together and making it happen. I always find it so interesting the way life has its twists and turns . . . some things just happen "Out of the Blue."

I am always amazed when I meet people and they speak of Kim, how the first thing they say is what a fantastic guitarist he was, but without fail, they always say how kind he always was and that he was one of the good guys. What a wonderful way to be remembered.

It was so important to Kim to finish this book so that he could share his experiences with me, his family, friends, and now, all of you. I'm so grateful he got to share his perspective on his life with us all. He continues to remind me that our lives are worth documenting, worth sharing with others, and worth living, because at the end of the day—it's all love.

Sending my love to you all, and know you have a piece of Kim's love with you as well. Thank you for reading his story. May it stay with you, for one day or for one hundred years.

## Eve Simmonds

Kim Simmonds was an incredible man. As his daughter, I think I'm qualified to speak on how incredible he truly was. The book you're holding in your hands was such a labor of love for him. This man never stopped sharing his art with the world, and it came to him in so many forms. The one we're all most familiar with is his love of music, which is how so many were introduced to him. He also had a love of painting and drawing, which he managed to share not only with the world, but within the walls of our home (there's still some stray paint marks on our ceiling from some late-night paint sessions!).

With all of that, I think the one form of his artistic talents that gets overlooked was his ability to write. He wrote so many lyrics, and many are poems in their own way. Writing was something he did every day—scribbles in little notebooks, lyrics on scrap pieces of paper, or even sending himself a text if a thought really caught him. It came so naturally to him. I guess I shouldn't have been that surprised when, out of the blue, he sent me an email with the subject "Chapter 1." This was the first chapter, and the first form of what eventually became this book.

It's such a privilege to have this book finally compiled. I have so many fond memories of getting his emails, which were always followed with phone calls where he would dive into his thought process. It's an even bigger privilege to share this with all of you—whether you're a longtime friend, a Savoy Brown superfan, or just hearing about Kim Simmonds for the first time, I think this book has something to share with you. The tidbits he shares about his life gave me so much context for the man I knew, and when I close my eyes, I can hear his voice so clearly in this book. The fact he decided to intimately open up about his life, and to give us a peek of what it was like through his perspective, opened up an entirely new side of him to me, and I hope it does the same for all of you.

Dad never stopped creating, using his iPad till the very end to paint landscapes in the hospital. Even now after his death, he continues to share his talents with us. Dad, I am so proud of you, and dear reader, I hope this book finds you exactly when you need it. The beautiful and tragic thing about being human is we get to be on this wondrous Earth for only a limited amount of time. Despite this, the art we create can live years beyond us . . .

maybe even decades, maybe even centuries. My father's art is now living beyond him and continues to find new audiences and find new meaning to those already familiar.

Thank you for reading, "mateys," and thank you for keeping the memory of my father alive and well. Rock and roll, and blues, forever.

## Friends

Savoy Brown was one of the bands on the scene when Free were breaking ground. A good band with a great guitarist, Kim Simmonds. His last album on Quarto Valley Records, released in 2023, *Blues All Around*, was a blues-rock-infused album with plenty of guts and determination woven into the songs. Savoy Brown was one of the bands that put England on the international music forefront.

—**Paul Rodgers**, singer and songwriter, Free, Bad Company, the Firm, and the Law

Kim was the consummate gentlemen and one hell of a guitarist. His feel and tone were steeped in American blues but with that classic British fire and elegance. He was a friend, and I miss him a lot. He would frequent my father's guitar shop in upstate New York. A nicer person in the music business would be hard to find in any era

—**Joe Bonamassa**, American blues-rock guitarist, singer, and songwriter

1967. I didn't get the job at my first audition. I got called back about a month later, borrowed Dad's car, and carried my drums up the stairs at the Nags Head Pub. We played for over two hours. As I'm packing up my kit, Kim says to me, "Where are you going; we have a gig in Birmingham tonight." That was the start of my long and fruitful friendship with Kim! I don't ever recall having a cross word with Kim. He trusted me with the sticks in his band.

Kim was constantly learning his craft. His intensity, power, and feel were magic. Especially live.

After leaving in 1971 and forming Foghat, we stayed in touch and were friends until the end. I invited him to play on our 2016 album, *Under the Influence,* which was a real joy for me and for Bryan and Scott (our guitaritsts).

During those recording sessions in Tennessee with producer Tom Hambridge, Kim said that he would love to write some songs for us. I told him that it would be great as long as you play on them!

Kim gifted us four songs that ended up on our *Sonic Mojo* album in November 2023. Unfortunately, due to illness, he could not make the recording sessions, but the songs did and became our first two singles. The fans loved them and so did we. Thank you, Kim.

I had the honor of inducting Kim into the New York Blues Hall of Fame at the Iridium in 2013.

Yes, an honor. We did get to play together many times over the years, especially the last ten years. It was always a gas to play with him. Fun, exciting, just great! Kim Simmonds was first and foremost a blues guitarist, a beautiful man, and a gentleman. I was fortunate to have played with Kim and call him my friend.

—**Roger Earl**, drummer, Savoy Brown and Foghat

Kim Simmonds was the most unassuming guy for a musician of his legend and stature that I've ever befriended.

In 2016, I was pushing to get Savoy Brown included on Rock Legends Cruise III with a who's who of rock icons: the Doobie Brothers, Dave Mason, Alice Cooper, Paul Rodgers, etc. Kim's response, in typical Kim fashion, was "Oh Tony, those are big stars . . . they're not going to want me on that bill!" Well, when the word got out that Kim Simmonds was indeed on the ship, he was sought out by all of them. The Doobie Brothers specially made sure he was invited in on their set, and their reverence for him was self-evident.

He stole the hearts of everyone on the cruise.

—**Tony Bullard**, guitarist, Earl and the Agitators

From the earliest days of Savoy Brown Blues Band, a group of very earnest young men rehearsing in an upstairs flat in Battersea, South London, to the last time we met, at the Edmonton Blues Festival, Canada, where he and the band were headlining, it's been a privilege to call Kim Simmonds a friend.

Savoy Brown had a multitude of personnel changes (there were three different lineups in the four years that I was a full-time member), but the one constant was the fluid, inventive, sparkling guitar playing that Kim brought to every occasion.

His creative outlook, always looking for new means of musical expression, propelled him to make changes to accompany his ever-expanding repertoire of original songs, whilst maintaining his unwavering connection to the blues music which was our original inspiration.

Although Kim and Savoy Brown had their major commercial successes in the States, Kim maintained a hard-core following of fans in the UK, and there were infrequent, but very enjoyable, band tours down the years in which I had the pleasure to sit in. I was also delighted to arrange a couple of solo tours for him around the turn of the century, for which my wife, Hilary, and I were his chauffeurs and privileged accompanists.

In 2004 I formed the British Blues All Stars, bringing together some of the best-known British blues artists of the sixties, and of course Kim was an integral part of that concept and was with us when we recorded our live album at Notodden Blues Festival.

Kim was always generous with his time, no more so than when in 2011, he gave Hilary and me ten days in his home studio to make an album, which he produced and on which he played some incredible solos. I couldn't be more proud of our efforts and was so glad to spend time with Kim, Debbie, and Eve at their home in Oswego.

We never know how time will treat us, or what our legacy will be, but I would not be at all surprised if Kim's reputation grows down the years, as I have met so many people who view him with affection, and so many musicians who say that Kim and Savoy Brown were their inspiration to take up an instrument. Certainly, he was one of the foremost creators of British blues and a unique irreplaceable talent.

—**Bob Hall**, British pianist and a member of Savoy Brown, collaborator of Alexi Korner, Dave and Jo-Ann Kelly, the Groundhogs Hall, worked and recorded with artists such as Peter Green and Danny Kirwan

I first became aware of Kim Simmonds on the evening of February 8, 1969. Kim was a great musician, but he was also a wonderful person. The two don't often go hand in hand, as I have learned. Kim was always accessible to fans, friendly and caring. If he liked you, nothing was held back. My friends Bob Schaffner and Mike Spencer were going to Europe and asked if they thought they could drop in and say hi to Kim in England. I asked Kim if it was OK, and he said, "Sure, have them come by." What is up with that! Too kind.

One thing that Kim and I shared was a love for the guitar playing of Peter Green and Danny Kirwan.

Some people become music fans for life. Some hear music and say, "Why couldn't I play like that?"

Kim was the latter. He had his guitar heroes he emulated: B.B. King, Albert King, Peter, and Danny, but then he took that inspiration, applied it to his own music, and then took it to a new level. Not many people can do that.

Also, he just couldn't quit. He wouldn't give up. Putting the guitar down was a nonstarter.

For him, music was like a riptide, a force so irresistible he just had to play. When the music is so strong in someone like Kim, that's when magic happens.

—**Paul Hamer**, American luthier, founder Hamer Guitars

Few people are lucky enough to befriend their childhood idols. I had that rare privilege, sharing a friendship with Kim for over forty years.

Achieving rock star status as a teenager was no accident for Kim. His curiosity, passion, and tenacity were the very forces that fueled his creativity.

I could spend hours talking about his extraordinary guitar playing and musical genius, but simply put—Kim was one of the greats. A pioneer in the music we all love called ROCK.

As a young musician, I idolized Kim Simmonds, the guitar player. As the years passed, I came to idolize Kim Simmonds, the human being.

A dear friend with a kind and gentle demeanor, Kim was the perfect blend of a complicated mind and a beautifully simple approach to life.

In his final words to me, Kim described himself in the most humble way: "Dean, I'm just a Blues Player . . . that's all I've ever been."

But to me, and to the millions he touched, Kim was so much more. I loved this Blues Player . . . and I always will.

—**Dean Zelinsky**, American luthier

Savoy Brown were an essential part of the late 1960s blues-rock family of bands in England, and I have fond memories of seeing them as a teenager at clubs like Eel Pie Island and Klooks Kleek, which was just down the road from their then home label Decca and its headquarters in north London.

Producer Mike Vernon had much to do with their early albums like *Shake Down*, *Getting to the Point*, *Blue Matter*, and *A Step Further,* which were very much a part of my album collection, and the live sides of the latter two famously captured the energy of the band's live performance. *Raw Sienna*, the next album release, presented some memorable compositions crafted by Kim Simmonds and Chris Youlden, who, sadly, left the band afterwards, and new lineups subsequently followed.

The band toured the US extensively throughout its life, and now living in Chicago, I saw many shows here when they came through. Most recently in St. Charles, Illinois, at a double bill with Foghat, and thus old bandmate Roger Earl and a chance to finally meet Kim (thank you, Bob), whom I have always thought was an unsung hero of the genre, with a very personal and distinctive sound and memorable style.

It is a testament to Kim's commitment to Savoy Brown and to loyal audiences worldwide that saw the band release forty-five albums over a period of fifty-eight years! No mean feat indeed!

Kim Simmonds passed in 2022 and, through Savoy Brown, leaves behind a fine catalog of work to discover and enjoy. Also, best wishes sent here to his wife, Debbie.

—**Michael Freeman**, April 2025 Grammy Award–winning producer, Keeping the Blues Alive Award recipient

Kim was so true to the blues and the boogie … he was one of the many giants from the UK who roamed the musical earth in those days-.Thank you, Kim.

—**Charlie Starr**, guitarist, Blackberry Smoke

# DISCOGRAPHY

## Savoy Brown Discography

*Shake Down*, Decca, 1967
*Getting to the Point*, Decca, 1968
*Blue Matter*, Decca, 1969
*A Step Further*, Decca, 1969
*Looking In*, Decca, 1970
*Raw Sienna*, Decca, 1970
*Street Corner Talking*, Decca, 1971
*Hellbound Train*, Decca, 1972
*Lion's Share*, Decca, 1972
*Jack the Toad*, Decca, 1973
*Boogie Brothers*, Decca, 1974
*Savoy Brown Featuring Kim Simmonds, Wire Fire*, London Records, 1975
*Skin 'n' Bone*, London Records, 1976
*Savage Return*, London Records, 1978
*Rock 'n' Roll Warriors*, Town House, Accord, 1981
*Greatest Hits Live in Concert*, Town House, 1981
*Just Live*, Line Records, 1981
*Live in Central Park*, Relix Records, 1985
*Slow Train*, Relix Records, 1986
*Make Me Sweat*, GNP Crescendo, 1988

*Kings of Boogie*, GNP Crescendo, 1989
*Live and Kickin'*, GNP Crescendo, 1990
*Let It Ride*, Roadhouse Music, Magnetic Air, SPV GmbH, 1992
*Bring It Home*, Viceroy Music Europe, 1994
*Live at the Record Plant*, Archive Recordings, 1998
*The Bottom Line Encore Collection*, the Bottom Line Record Company, LLC, BMG Distribution, 1999
*The Blues Keep Me Holding On*, Mystic Music & Entertainment, 1999
*Looking from the Outside, Live '69 & '70*, Mooncrest, 2000
*Jack the Toad, Live 70/72*, Mooncrest, 2000
*Strange Dreams*, Blind Pig Records, 2003
*You Should Have Been There*, Panache Records, 2004
*Steel*, Panache Records, 2007
*Too Much of a Good Thing*, 2009
*Voodoo Moon*, Ruf Records, 2011
*Songs from the Road*, Ruf Records, 2013
*Goin' to the Delta*, Ruf Records, 2014
*The Devil to Pay*, Ruf Records, 2015
*Still Live After 50 Years, Volume 1*, Panache Records, 2017
*Witchy Feelin'*, Ruf Records, 2017
*City Night*, Quarto Valley Records, 2019
*Still Live After 50 Years, Volume 2*, Panache Records, 2019
*Ain't Done Yet*, Quarto Valley Records, 2020
*Blues All Around*, Quarto Valley Records, 2023

## Kim Simmonds' Solo LPs

*Solitaire*, 1997
*Blues Like Midnight*, 2001
*Struck by Lightning*, 2004
*Out of the Blue*, 2008
*Jazzin' on the Blues*, 2015

*Voodoo Moon*, *Goin' to the Delta*, *The Devil to Pay*, and *Witchy Feelin'* are now all owned by Panache Records. All solo recording are also owned by Panache.

# ACKNOWLEDGMENTS

A big thank-you and much love to our daughter, Eve Simmonds, for her unwavering support, input, and help for both her dad and me.

Thank you to our dear friend Tony Bullard for putting the pieces together for me.

Huge thanks to Robert Schaffner, who has been instrumental in getting this book published and has also become a good friend. I truly could not have done it without him.

Long-standing thanks to Pat DeSalvo and Garnet Grimm, who have been two of the best bandmates, musicians, and friends to Kim and me that anyone could ever ask for.

Thank you to John Shelmet for all you do and being a sounding board, confidante, and very good friend to Kim and supporter and facilitator to me. I so appreciate it.

Thank you to Linda Arcello Earl for her unwavering willingness to mentor, help, guide, and advise.

Thank you to our good friend Bruce Quarto of Quarto Valley Records, who has been a wonderful partner to Kim and Savoy Brown these past years.

Thank you to Schiffer Publishing and Bob Biondi to make this a reality to help carry on my husband's legacy.

And to all who contributed to this book in whatever way, I thank you so much.

# INDEX